BURMA MY MOTHER

And Why I Had to Leave

Sao Khemawadee Mangrai

Second print book edition: Sydney, 2016.
Publisher: Sydney School of Arts & Humanities
15-17 Argyle Place Millers Point NSW 2000 Australia

www.ssoa.com.au

ISBN: 978-0-9945441-8-6

First published 2014.

Cover image:
Portrait in 1932 of Khemawadee's mother by Sir Gerald Kelly, portrait painter to the British royal family.

Dedication

To my parents, Sao Khun Mong & Sao Ohn Nyunt, my husband, Hom, my children, Seng, Orawan, Mani & Art, my brothers, and my cousins, nephews and nieces, who have been deprived of their heritage by the military government.

Acknowledgements

My thanks to my family, to my many friends who have shared my experience of living in Burma, and to my new friends in Australia.

I would like to acknowledge the wholehearted encouragement I was given by fellow members of OMG! (Our Memoir Group) meeting at Ampersand Cafe, Surry Hills, and the Sydney School of Arts & Humanities in Redfern, Sydney. I owe the members many thanks for listening patiently, for giving me ideas to add to my writing, and for their support.

I'm forever indebted to Dr Christine Williams for conducting the memoir writing course that I attended and for guiding and driving me through the process of writing, and for her editing and her patience. I'm equally grateful to Kay Barker who typed the stories from my handwritten pages despite all the unfamiliar Shan & Burmese names.

I want to acknowledge with gratitude the backroom people behind this publication: Jeremy Gilling for proofreading, Syam Sudhakar, Faisal Sayani and Ferdinando Manzo for creating the cover designs, Nick Waters for transforming the manuscript into an e-book format, and Vernon Song for building and managing the website for the book's sale. Thanks also to Chris Waters for my bio photograph and all the members of my family who provided illustrations, especially Maung Maung Than and *shanwomen.org*.

Finally, my greatest appreciation goes to my husband for being a walking dictionary and for encouraging me to attend the memoir course to write about our family. Great thanks also to my children who have supported me along the way.

Author biography

Sao Khemawadee means 'worry-free' but she has led a life far from being free of cares. She was born in Hsipaw, in the northern Shan states of Burma, and spent her youth there and later in Rangoon, as a university tutor. She married and raised four children, her future father-in-law was killed alongside General Aung San during a Cabinet meeting, and her husband was later imprisoned. She and her family left their homeland to live in Fiji before migrating to Australia in 1991. A Buddhist, Sao Khemawadee carries out traditional religious practices and regularly attends the Yennora monastery in Sydney.

Contents

Foreword

When Khemawadee first appeared as a student in a writing course I conducted in Sydney, I realised she had a treasure trove of stories of her former life in Burma held securely in her memory. One day she quietly told me, almost as an aside, that she hoped to be able to complete a memoir before she died. From that moment, we formed a kind of silent pact that her fascinating and valuable life stories would one day find a home, to be showcased to the reading public. Events unfolded. The students of that memoir group decided to form a weekly gathering, the genesis of OMG! (Our Memoir Group) in Sydney, which has persisted for over four years. A miracle in itself! Khemawadee's ebook is the first of several which will be produced this year by Sydney School of Arts & Humanities, with the prospect of further works by developing writers to come.

Once our group had settled into our principle venue, the **'&'** cafe in Surry Hills, advice flowed and several members took on the responsibility of typing or emailing as required. I can only thank our lucky stars that Khemawadee and I have both stayed the distance required to produce such a simultaneously personal and worldly account of her remarkable life, lived according to Buddhist principles within a political landscape of repression and a background of an ancient and rich cultural heritage which is fast being lost to us all.

Khemawadee recalls the beauty and grace of a way of life steeped in religious ritual and regal ceremony, complete with pagodas and precious jewels, thatched roofs and geckoes, chilli and ginger, even orchids and lotuses.

From her account of surviving a raid on her home by Allied bombers during WWII, to the harrowing story of her family hiding in caves in the jungle in order to escape the Japanese, to the report of the assassination of her husband's father, to the description of his own imprisonment by the military government for five years before the family's self-exile – all these stories are told with simplicity and understatement. Khemawadee is not one to get herself into a flap over trivialities.

For all that the author might have justification to feel bitter about many horrific events in her life, including the loss of friends and compatriots, there's a quality of compassion, forbearance and wisdom which infuses her writing. Her truths, as well as her triumphs over adversity, are evident in this story of a gentle exile from Myanmar.

Dr Christine Williams

BHUTAN
INDIA
CHINA
BANGLADESH
Kachin
Sagaing
Maymyo
Shan
Chin
Mandalay
Mandalay
Taunggyi
Rakhine
LAOS
Magway
Kayah
Bago
Yangon
Kayin
Ayeyarwady
Yangon
THAILAND
Mon
Tanintharyi

Chapter 1

Born and bred in Burma – my early years

Some of my ancestors, including my mother (front row third from the left)

HISTORY OF HSIPAW STATE

Written by

Mg Kalinda,
Shan Teacher,
Myo Lai Gr
Hsipaw

Genealogy document of the Hsipaw state

\Come in close to me, reader, and let me tell you about myself – as I am now, and as I was, my life shaped according to the times I've lived through.

I am who I am because I'm a Monday-born, having arrived in the world on 5 October 1937 at 7.10 pm. My Zodiac sign is Libra, and according to Burmese astrology, my birth sign is a 'Tiger', showing the following attributes: intelligence, intuition, strength and patience. I can only hope so. It's also said that I'm goal-oriented, I like to succeed but I'm respectful of laws, and that I take responsibility for my actions. As a 'Tiger', I don't believe I'm a fearsome creature ... perhaps more a kitten.

I don't have a birth certificate. On the other hand, I have a dried palm leaf on which my individual birth signs – the day, date and hour – along with the astrological signs, are written with a stylus. My name, Sao Khemawadee, was chosen according to the day of my birth, but when I was a baby an Australian woman who was a friend of the family, Winnie McDonough, gave me the name 'Biddy' when she spotted me, and it stuck – for life. It was only at high school when I had to fill in official forms and was addressed by teachers that I was known as Khemawadee. Everyone else has always called me 'Biddy' and I'm happy with that among friends.

My coming into this world didn't make as great an impact as my brother's birth had done. He was a first-born son whereas I was a baby girl and a second child, with less status. When my older brother Tony was about to be born, drivers were not allowed to toot their horns when driving around the estate where we lived in case my mother became alarmed, and the rule continued to apply after he was born, as his sleep could have been disturbed by the noise. No one worried whether I slept or not.

Evening-born is not as good as morning-born for good fortune in life, according to Burmese beliefs – and I was told from my earliest years that I was born in the evening. The story goes that when my mother was pregnant with me, she would take a walk every evening with her two brothers-in-law. They were my father's brothers Sao Sai Mong and Sao Khun Suik. While still at school they had been my father's best men at my parents' wedding, as they used to spend school holidays with my parents because their own home town was too far away to travel to and from school in Maymyo.

On one particular evening before her walk my mother had taken a dose of Eno, an effervescent antacid to relieve indigestion and nausea. But she had to cut short that evening walk when she thought the Eno was working too well. She rushed home, only to find that the reason she was feeling upset in the stomach was that I was in a hurry to come out into the world. My mother didn't have time to get into the main house so the quarters assigned to the maids had to be cleaned in haste to serve as a labour room. The midwife was called in and there I was – born in the servant's quarters! This contributed to the shape of things to come. And ever after I was called 'the Eno baby'.

I believe in astrology, mythology, and celestial and supernatural beings, as most Burmese do. I don't shun superstitions, fortune tellers and psychics. In fact, I consult fortune tellers and psychics when I am faced with quandaries such as when I sit exams, when any of my children or my husband go for job interviews, or when they are very sick. Consultation is followed up with prayers and antidotes, and I carry them out religiously. I always follow advice on what must be done to avert an impending event or to bring about what one desires. Most of the time it works. If it doesn't, I just take it in my stride and accept my fate gracefully.

I was brought up and educated as an ordinary student. I wouldn't have had it any other way though. By contrast, my mother's two younger sisters, both around sixteen years older than me – Aunty Millie and Aunty Pansy – were given special treatment at school, the same school that I attended some years later in 1947 where I was treated just like all the other students. I even went to less-than-ordinary primary schools.

During the Japanese occupation in Burma in World War II, the people of our village, Hsum Hsai, had to flee and hide deep in the jungle. There I attended a semblance of a school in caves, the students sitting on a rocky ledge under the protection of a protruding slab of rock. We had a teacher who taught us the Burmese alphabet and our older aunt taught us the English alphabet.

Once the war was over, we went back to our village where I attended a school built on stilts with a flattened bamboo floor, matted bamboo walls and a thatched roof. We had to sit on the bamboo mats. There was only one teacher. He was a chubby and good-natured man who taught the six-to-ten year olds at the village school. The day would start with chanting Burmese Buddhist prayers. During the lunch break we would explore the surrounding area. There was a whitewashed pagoda, the four sides of which had niches in which marble statues of a sitting Buddha were installed. Nearby was a huge banyan tree where birds rested and nested. The undergrowth was damp and strewn with yellow banyan fruits. At night the brown fish owl would make a sound, 'doodoo dee dee doodoo'. The gecko would cry 'ga ratat tat taukhe', the word 'tau te' (pronounced with a 'k' sound) being the name of that lizard. My younger brothers and I would huddle together whenever we heard those sounds from across the road at night because we'd been told spooky stories about owls, and also that the gecko would stick to your neck, not releasing itself until thunder struck.

Not far away from the banyan tree was a shed made of timber posts and a corrugated iron roof. It had a two-foot-high brick enclosure around it with an opening to walk through to indicate that people should show reverence as they approached. In the centre of the shed, mounted on concrete bases, were human-sized statues depicting states of pain and suffering. One depicted old age as a bent and shrunken old man leaning on a walking stick. Another showed a man wracked with pain. The most frightening statue was of a man lying on his back with a bloated stomach on which sat a vulture feasting on the man's innards with part of an intestine dangling from its beak. This was to convey a message that in Buddhism, ageing, suffering, pain and death are inevitable. For nine and ten-year-olds it had an eerie effect and gave me nightmares for some time.

By about this time, when I was ten, it was decided that I needed better primary schooling, so I was sent with my Aunty Pansy to live with my father's old teacher and his family. I had to stay with them until the boarding house of St Joseph's convent in Maymyo was rebuilt after having been damaged by bombing during the war.

I don't know whether Dad did the right thing sending his only daughter to live with his old teacher's family. The teacher had a granddaughter, Kathleen, with whom I made daily trips to the convent school together with his niece, Pansy, and my Aunty Pansy. We travelled in a horse-drawn cart known as a *gharry* about a kilometre every day to school until my aunt left for Mandalay after about a year. She had to attend pre-matriculation classes to make up for not having gone to school during World War II. I missed my aunt and I missed home. About a month later, we were joined by two more nieces of my father's old teacher who were much older than his granddaughter and me. They took me under their wings and bathed me, washed my clothes and hair, and made my bed for me. This was some consolation to me for being so far away from my mother, yet I still longed to be with her.

We used to wear as our school uniforms pinafores made out of silky nylon parachute fabric since the war was only recently ended and uniform materials were scarce. We had to undo the stitches and use the same thread for making our skirts. When Aunty Pansy first left for Mandalay, I felt abandoned among strangers. From then on I had to fend for myself. I learnt to respect other people's possessions and to watch others' facial expressions closely. I became timid.

Our bed linen and heavy clothing used to be washed by the *dhobi* who came every week to collect them, bringing them back the following week. Someone had to make a list of the washing items and we would use a stump of a pencil kept in a book between the pages for the previous and the latest list. One day I was about to leave for school when I found that I didn't have a pencil. I just grabbed the pencil from the *dhobi* list and ran to board the *gharry*. Towards evening, after getting home from school, the *dhobi* came and the whole household was looking for the pencil. I hurried to retrieve it from my schoolbag and produce it for whoever was making the list. The old woman pointed her finger at me, calling me a thief. From that day on I refrained from touching other people's possessions.

In the evenings when the homework was done, Kathleen, her maid or companion, who was about our age, and I would entertain ourselves. We would take turns to dance, and when it was my turn, as I stooped, bent knees and arms in time with the beat, they started laughing at me for not making the right movements. Can you imagine me making those sinuous movements? Burmese dancing needs supple fingers and hands and an agility of the body. So that was the end of my dancing performances. My whole family – my parents and five brothers – dance beautifully, whether ballroom, jive, cha cha cha, rumba or samba. I couldn't do any, except a waltz with my father, who used to lead me so that I felt safe in his arms.

I can remember one day in 1947, when I was nine, my father's teacher telling me about the assassination in Rangoon of General Aung San, who was the leader of Burma's independence movement which was seeking freedom from British rule. The teacher asked me if I was related to the Shan chief Sao Sam Htun, who was assassinated with him. I told him I was not. How was I to know that my life would take a course which years later would bring me close to the centre of Burmese political life, with a strong connection to Sao Sam Htun's family?

Still a girl at this stage, I continued on with my simple life. After about a year in the home of my father's teacher, when I was about eleven, the boarding department of the convent was ready to take in boarders for the first time since the building's reconstruction. I was placed in the small girls' dormitory and I was quite happy living, playing and studying with the girls of my age. We used to play in the school grounds, rolling down slopes cushioned by pine needles, and swinging on the parallel bars and ring bars meant for the butlers, as well as the swings installed for us. We would swing high 'to reach the sky'.

I remember how much we used to enjoy gathering around a hawker who had a variety of sweetmeats laid out on a big brass tray which he carried on his head, balanced on a coil of cloth. We loved watching another seller who had colourful ribbons, hair clips and bows spread out on a cloth on the ground to sell. We bought whatever we fancied to adorn our hair when we went on Saturday evening walks. We would walk side by side in a line.

Sometimes we would walk to nearby strawberry fields where we could help ourselves to as many strawberries as we could pick and eat, as long as we didn't trample all over the patches.

We also used to go to an in-ground swimming pool outside of the school grounds which was part of the property of a family who processed coffee sold throughout Burma, coffee which was sought after by tourists for its high quality.

For the Christmas holidays in 1948, I stayed, along with my cousin Gladys, at a coffee plantation about thirty kilometres from my school because my family home was too far to travel for the ten-day break. The owners of the coffee plantation were Mr & Mrs Forbes, an English couple. Their cook and his wife came to fetch us at the school and we travelled part of the journey by car on a main road and part of it by bullock cart along a jungle track. The plantation was a beautiful place. We would wake up to the sound of birds singing and twittering while they ate red, ripe coffee beans.

I remember clearly the next Christmas holidays staying with my grandmother in Hsum Hsai because my parents had moved again. To return to St Joseph's convent school, I was put in a jalopy which carried milk cans to Maymyo, about thirty kilometres away, together with a woman related to my father's assistant who was going shopping there. A slow uphill trip, it was uncomfortable and I had to be careful I wasn't crushed by one of the ten milk cans on board if any fell over. It was a tight fit.

The following Christmas we waited for the cook and his wife from the plantation to come and fetch us. They did come, but only to break the shocking news to us that the plantation owners had been killed brutally by a group who called themselves members of the Burma Communist Party. Burma had gained independence in 1948 and was under a parliamentary government. Some people chose not to recognise this government and went underground. They were both anti-government and anti-British. We were saddened by the news but thankful that it hadn't taken place while we were on holiday at the plantation. I shudder when I think what might have been our fate.

The following holiday we went home to my birthplace. It was my mother's principality, as she was the sister-in-law of the second-last chief of Hsipaw state. He hadn't produced an heir so my father had been appointed by the British to take over the administration of the state. This meant great responsibility and a great deal of work for my mother as the administrator's wife ... besides looking after her six children. At least she had a cook and other servants. I felt happy to be back with my mother, but our home felt a little strange because it was much more grand than our former simple home.

I remember how we as schoolgirls had led happy, simple lives up until Burma gained its long-fought-for independence from British rule on 4 January 1948. At first people all over Burma rejoiced; they looked forward to peace and prosperity. But soon rebellions among ethnic groups broke out. I remember when one group calling itself the Karen National Defence Organisation took over most of Lower Burma. The town where we went to school, Maymyo, named after a British army officer, James May, was surrounded by the rebels and a battle took place between the government troops and the Karen troops.

I believe that one of the earliest plane hijackings in Asia took place in the early 1950s when a Union of Burma Airways plane was taken over by a rebel Karen officer who ordered the pilot to fly to the Irrawaddy Delta, which was at that time occupied by Karen rebels. The plane was carrying pay packages for government employees, and I don't think the money was ever recovered. Earlier, in 1946 when my husband was a boy aged about eleven, the hijacker had been his tutor in English.

But I had not even reached adolescence when this political turmoil began, and before I tell you anything more about my youth, I need to go back a little way into the extraordinary history of my forebears. So let's start with some family history.

Chapter 2

My mother and grandmother

*Three generations: Sao Khemawadee,
her mother Sao Ohn Nyunt and grandmother Khin Padauk*

Born on 14 March 1909, Mum was named Sao Ohn Nyunt, meaning 'tender shoot of a coconut palm'. She was adopted by her uncle, Sir Sao Khe, because her father, Sao Lu, had died while she was still in her mother's womb.

It was a big group of children all brought up together, their names sounding like a roll call: Mum's sister, Sao Thu Nandar; her older cousins Sao Kyar Nyunt, Sao Ohn Mar, Sao Thiri Marlar; Sao Intra, the son of Sao Kawn Kiao Intaleng, chief of Kengtung; and also the daughters of my mother's younger uncle, Sao O, who were named Sao Wunna and Ma Ma Galay.

Except for one younger cousin, my mother was about nine years younger than most of the others. I can imagine she must have been quite lonely. Then, about ten years later, her two younger sisters, my Aunty Millie and Aunty Pansy, were born after my grandmother married her father's best friend, U Mg Mg Ba, an advisor to the chief, Sir Sao Khe. My two aunties were sent to St Joseph's convent in Maymyo, and my mum was also sent there later to learn to speak English.

Mum's elder sister Sao Thu Nandar married her cousin Sao Ohn Kyar, son of the chief, and in 1932 they visited England to attend the Round Table Conference at St James's Palace. My mum went along too. At one luncheon party she happened to be seated next to the artist Sir Gerald Kelly, a portrait painter to the British royal family. She was asked whether she was bored being left alone while her sister and brother-in-law attended luncheon and dinner parties. When she replied that she was quite bored, he asked if she would like to sit for him. She consented and he made fourteen drawings as work towards painting eight portraits.

About thirty years later, my dad saw a print of one of the paintings in a 1956 issue of *The Illustrated London News*. The caption said 'Sao Ohn Nyunt the Burmese dancer'. Dad was annoyed that his wife was described as a dancer. He at once wrote to Sir Gerald Kelly that Sao Ohn Nyunt was not a dancer but a princess. I suppose the confusion arose because in Burmese the word 'minthamee' means a dancer or a princess. Dad also wrote that Sao Ohn Nyunt was alive and married, that she had six children and lived in Lashio, Shan state, Burma. The outcome was that Sir Gerald Kelly sent Mum and Dad two prints with his signature on them, and six more prints for each of their offspring.

Kelly, portrait painter to the British royal family, and one of his eight portraits of my mother

I've been told that by 1968, 36,000 prints or copies had been sold. My mother was publicly described as a wistful girl and a shy, lonely and delicate creature, endowed by nature and by her princess-like upbringing with grace and serenity. Yes, she had grace and serenity. Dad would always describe her as petite. He would call her by the name she'd been given in her convent school, Jean, and was always very proud to be her husband.

In April 2011, at last one of the original paintings of my mother was brought back from London to its spiritual home, Myanmar, seventy-nine years after it was painted. A keen Burmese businessman, Thet Paing Soe, negotiated with the Maas Gallery of Mayfair, London, to buy the portrait which its owner, Rupert Maas, had bought from a private collection in the United States in 2003. He is reported in *The Myanmar Times* to have said that when the painting arrived, he sat in front of it the whole night, just 'gazing, gazing and gazing at her'.

'For me, it was a dream come true; my joy is immeasurable,' he is quoted as saying.

The article said my mother had 'as much of a royal background as any princess in a fairytale'.

Her grandfather Sao Hkun Hseng was the *sawbwa* (Shan king) of Hsipaw from 1866 to 1902, and his Maha Devi was a princess royal of the Konbaung dynasty (1752-1885).[1]

I have only a print of one of the sketches as well as prints of two paintings in the series – a pink and a yellow *htamein* –

and all these prints on paper are now worn with age. Oh, how I would love to own an original. At one time it was suggested that all of Mum's children might contribute to the cost of one of the paintings, but of course, now, having lost most of our property in Burma because we had to leave in self-exile, we cannot afford to buy any of the paintings.

At least I have seen one of the originals with my own eyes. In 2013 Thet Paing Soe invited me to his home in Rangoon for a viewing, telling me that since he'd been very young he'd always wanted to buy the painting. At least I feel it's safe in his hands, that he will take good care of my mother's portrait.

At the end of the 1932 trip, my mother had been left behind in London in the guardianship of the vicar and his wife. Then she was sent to a 'finishing school' in Switzerland. She learnt to cook and paint. I never knew that she had lived in Switzerland and that she could paint until one of her classmates sent her grandson to Burma to look for my mother in Lashio in the early years of this century. By that time Mum had already passed away, as she died in 2003, but he was able to make contact with my brother, Sydney, who gave him one of my mother's paintings. That was how I came to know about her days abroad. Since I was the only daughter, we might have been close, but as all we children were sent to boarding schools and only came home during the holidays, we did not have time to share our life experiences. I regret that I had not asked her about her father, her adoptive father and her stepfather.

My father and mother were married on 20 April 1934. It was not an arranged marriage – they loved each other. My father adored my mother and she worshipped him. She was patient with him, standing by him for more than fifty years: through the jobless months, surviving World War II, moving from place to place as the wife of an administrator and an executive engineer, the manager of a match factory and a car business, hardly ever losing her temper.

I did see her lose her temper once, early one morning on a full moon day of the month. As was usual, Mum would get up early on the Sabbath day. Burmese Buddhists get up about four in the morning to prepare fresh fruits and cook rice to be able to offer them to the Buddha before sunrise. They would say prayers and share merits with the living, the dead, the spirits – good or bad – and all creatures. This particular morning the maids were not up yet, so the rice wasn't cooked and the fruits were not ready. Mum was really very angry. When my aunt Sao Bo Sawan, Dad's sister, saw Mum reading while her own sons were playing loudly nearby, she asked Mum, 'How can you go on reading while your sons are playing so noisily nearby?' Mum replied, 'I've already told them to be quiet once. Since they don't listen, let them be.' She would always let us children make noise, leaving it to my father to discipline us, but this time was different. It was the greatest show of anger I ever saw, and even so, it wasn't much. I don't remember her ever saying a harsh word to me – she was an even-tempered woman.

In this she was like her own mother, sharing a quality that ran in the family. My mother was one of four daughters to my grandmother, Khin Padauk, who was named after the clusters of yellow flowers of a local tree. In order, the girls were: Sao Thu Nandar (meaning 'good and beautiful), then my mother, then Khin Ma Gyi (meaning 'older', and later known to me as Aunty Millie), and last, Khin Ma Lay (meaning 'younger', later known as Aunty Pansy).

The three youngest girls were educated at St Joseph's Convent in Maymyo at the expense of the Hsipaw state. They went to the university and pre-university. But after World War II, my grandmother did not think it was necessary for Pansy and Millie to complete their tertiary education. We can't put my grandmother down as a narrow-minded person. She just wanted her daughters to be near her as their father had passed away. But in 1935 her eldest daughter ran away with a dancer, leaving what was described as 'the chief's protection,' and later Aunty Millie also eloped with a clerk, but that relationship turned out to be a good match.

At first my grandmother was the only wife of my grandfather Sao Lu, but later she learnt to get along with his four other wives. As she grew older my Aunty Millie went to live with her.

It was at an amazing age that my grandmother passed away in 1973. She was ninety-five and was active up until close to her death. At the time I was aged about thirty-six, and all my life I'd known my grandmother as someone who'd liked sweeping, cleaning, weeding, and reading newspapers from the front page to the back. Even at this age she did not need spectacles. As far as I could recollect she was never ill or bedridden except for a slight cold or a bit of fever. If she had not slipped and hit her head against the toilet bowl while scrubbing the bathroom floor, she may have lived to the age of a hundred. Even at ninety-two, she still liked going to the cinema to see her favourite actors' films.

It was my grandmother Khin Padauk who taught me most of my Buddhist prayers. It was she who made me pretty rag dolls, using wax to stiffen the cloth to be able to form noses and mouths. She would sew clothes for her other grandchildren on a manual Singer sewing machine.

Every night my grandmother would have tamarind and jaggery (palm sugar). She rolled it into a marble-sized ball and swallowed this, whole, for laxative purposes. Then she would sit on the floor, stretch her legs and do toe-touching exercises before she went to bed.

She smelt sweet. After her bath she would apply white sandalwood and smother sweet-smelling red and brown sandalwood paste all over her body and dust herself with Yardley body powder. She also sprayed Yardley lavender perfume on herself. She would put on a bodice with sleeves, a singlet and a petticoat on top of one another, and a white under-*longyi* and a printed *longyi* or sarong with a matching organza jacket buttoned at the side. There was a little pocket under the overlapping flap to place a watch which she took out and put back into her pocket to keep track of time.

But as she aged she lost track of time. She was able to indulge her weakness for cards, playing with her friends for small stakes for hours, with the maids periodically bringing them all tea. By then my grandmother had no household duties to perform.

In her eighties, she would sit there on the carpeted floor from lunchtime through teatime and dinnertime, until dawn. She and her friends would be served dinner on a low round table. She did not have to worry about children. There were always distant relatives or cousins who were happy enough to look after the children, to cook and keep house. They were pleased to be given a place to live and be clothed. In fact, it was regarded as prestigious to be living in town, at the court.

After my grandmother died, she was cremated. Her coffin was placed on a pile of firewood and sandalwood, and ghee was then poured onto the pile and lit. The ceremony, performed at a cemetery in Lashio, was a heart-wrenching occasion and the first death in the family that I had experienced. All four of my grandmother's daughters, plus her ten grandchildren, attended. I remember my mother being her own calm self.

She was very different, though, once when she visited Kengtung from Lashio in the 1950s. My mother's sister-in-law, Sao Bo Sawan, gave her a gold bar at the airport as she was about to leave, just to help her with some extra money since she had a big family. According to my aunt, Mum turned white and lost her composure entirely. My aunt scolded her, saying 'Sao Ohn Nyunt, be natural, be yourself.' But my mother was worried that the gold might be stolen or taken at the customs desk, so she hugged her handbag close to her chest as she boarded the plane. My aunt would sometimes send clothes such as Hawaiian shirts and batik sarongs that came across the border from Thailand, which my aunt would have bought for Mum to sell in Lashio. Mum would give the clothes to shopkeepers on credit for which she would receive nothing in return. She was vulnerable by then.

I remember when I was young looking forward to seeing Mum as the end of the school term approached. As soon as the last class finished at four o'clock, Dad's assistant engineer would come to drive us home. My brothers and I would ask him to drive all night, we were so impatient to get home. Dad's assistant's name was Mr Johnson and he weighed about 90 kilos, and his wife and his son always accompanied him. On one trip we were driving at dusk past a place about halfway along the journey, and we asked him if he wanted to stop there for the night. He promptly refused since the bungalow was surrounded by banyan trees and he believed it was haunted. He said he had found himself one morning with his bed turned the other way around. Imagine, who could have moved it with him sleeping on it with his heavy bodyweight? Anyway, he drove on. It was safe to travel at night in those days, the 1950s. No insurgents and highway robbers – no dangers except tigers. One night a lone tiger was sitting in the middle of the road, his eyes reflecting the light from the headlights of the jeep we were travelling in. Thankfully the animal moved away and disappeared into the dark jungle.

Eventually we arrived at Lashio at 3 am. The front door of our house burst open and my mother's face lit up with a smile that touched our hearts. It was a smile that we, her children, will never forget. 'I knew you would be arriving today,' she said. She loved us all but we knew that she loved three of her children more than the rest of us. They were her eldest and her youngest, plus her special favourite, her fourth child, Tim, who would cling to her sarong when she took us to school. He was sent to Edinburgh when he was fourteen on a scholarship and never returned. She was never to see him again.

In the face of many hardships, my mum would always act with grace and press on with her work. She was an excellent cook, baking cakes for afternoon tea and making desserts for dinner. Our favourites were lemon meringue and jam tarts. We didn't like trifles or mango and papaya pulp dishes. She cooked Shan or Burmese food for lunch and western food for dinner. She was also expert in knitting. She knitted clothing, especially woollen socks, the whole year round for Dad and the six of us. She was also a keen gardener. She and her best friends compared notes and showed off to each other their newly acquired plants, found in markets and on road trips through the forests. She travelled all over the Shan states with Dad, and when passing through forests she was always on the lookout for orchids. The spare driver would climb a tree and bring down the orchids, and Mum would add them to her collection in the orchid house.

When Dad passed away in April 1985 from heart failure, she lost all interest in life. Her days had revolved around Dad and she stopped cooking, she stopped knitting, and lost interest in everyone except those of us in her family. Once he was gone she lost her energy and sense of purpose. Her rheumatoid arthritis set in. At least she kept on reading, even after an eye operation. Diabetes, an enlarged heart and high blood pressure finally took her life in 1995, in the same month ten years after Dad had died.

I couldn't go home to Burma for my mother's funeral rites from Sydney where I was living at the time, as we had applied for refugee status and our travel documents were not yet in order. Mum had lived with us in Fiji for four years. When she'd wanted to return home to live in Burma in 1990, we took her as far as Bangkok and asked her to stay there, living with my brother Sydney, until my husband, Hom, might be assigned by the UN to another posting, closer to Burma. But she couldn't wait to go home as she missed her sisters and she missed her youngest son, Gerry, most of all. She lived with him for four years until she passed away.

I think she must have been quite satisfied with her life because her youngest son had just moved into a newly built government house and she would have thought her son was doing well. But for my sake, I regret that I left her in Bangkok with my brother Sydney. I regret that I didn't leave her a return air ticket so that she could join us here in Australia. It was not until two years after her death that I was issued with an Australian citizen's passport, allowing me to travel to Rangoon to float an urn which held her ashes down the Hlaing River, a tributary of the Irrawaddy. The floating ceremony was organised to follow on from alms and food being given to the monks, and a meal provided for friends and relatives to share the merits with them. The urn had been left in the care of the monks at the monastery, near our house, for two years.

We had to carry the urn to the bank of the Hlaing River where there was a boat. Our son held onto a post at the bow of the boat and slowly lowered the urn down into the river. At last, once the urn floated down the river, I felt that her spirit had been released and she was able to go anywhere she fancied.

The Burmese believe that seven days after a person's death, after the merrymaking and prayers have been completed, the spirit of that person can go anywhere they like. This period of confinement after Mum's death had lasted three years while I was waiting for travel documents to be issued without affecting my success in an application for Australian citizenship, so it was a great relief to feel that my mother was set free at last.

Still, all this while, I've felt sad because she hasn't visited me in my dreams. In Sydney when I think of her, I know that both of my parents would have loved the life here, so at least I feel she is happy that I'm living in Sydney. And writing this book has helped me to connect with her again.*My mother, Sao*

Ohn Nyunt (on right), and her sister, Sao Thu Nandar

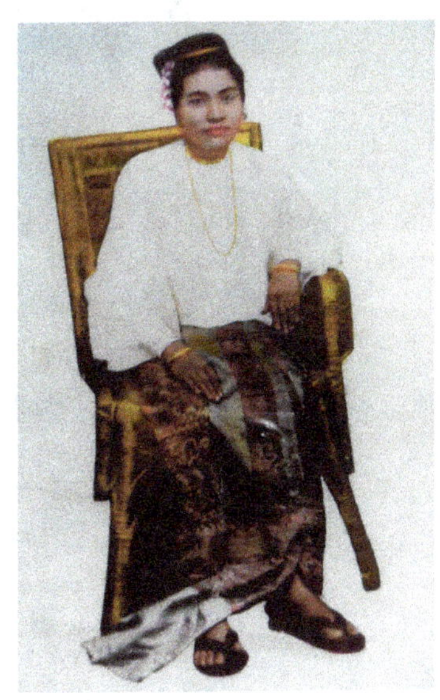

My grandmother Khin Padauk

Chapter 3

My father

My father in the early 1950s

Dad's name was Sao Khun Mong Mangrai. He was born in 1905, a descendent of King Mangrai and the fourth son of the 38th chief of Kengtung state.

His name means 'lord of the state'. However, he was not destined to be a chief. Being the fourth son, he was by no means eligible for chieftainship, so he was sent to Maymyo to attend a government school. There he was given the name Leslie as students were required to have an English name. He was joined by his brothers Sao Sai Mong, whose name didn't change as it showed his link with his state, and Sao Khun Suik, known as Dennis.

During school holidays all three had to go to Hsipaw, the capital of the northern Shan states, 220 kilometres from Mandalay in central Burma. It was about sixty-eight kilometres away from Maymyo – a shorter distance than going back to his home in Kengtung, which was four days' travel by road during his childhood, in fact right up until the 1950s.

The reason they could go to Hsipaw was that my father's eldest brother, Sao Kawng Tai, had married the Hsipaw chief's eldest daughter, and my father's third-oldest brother was also adopted by the Hsipaw chief as he had only one son. So there had already been a strong connection established between the two states, Kengtung, an eastern Shan state, and Hsipaw, a northern Shan state, before my father was introduced into the equation.

When my father's eldest brother, Sao Kawng Tai, became the 39th chief of the largest state, Kentung, he became a powerful figure considering the links he already had with Hispaw state. He was seven days older than Sao Hpom Li, who thought he was the rightful heir to the Kengtung chieftainship as he was the son of another of the chief's wives, the current Mahadevi. This resentment must have brewed in him for years, as later events would show.

By the age of about twenty-five my father was sent to England to study mining engineering at the Royal School of Mines. What a life he must have had in London! He would teach ballroom dancing whenever he ran out of pocket money.

In the meantime, my mother went along with her older sister, Sao Thu Nandar, on a trip to London. Her sister was accompanying her husband, Sao Ohn Kyar, the then chief of Hsipaw state, who was invited to attend the 1932 Round Table Conference at St James's Court – one of several conferences held over three years, 1930-1932, to discuss constitutional reforms of British rule in India and surrounding states.

My father met my mother in London, but I don't know whether they'd already met back in Burma when he used go home for holidays. After the conference, when my aunt returned to Burma, my mother stayed on with friends, a vicar and his wife, to learn to speak English well. Perhaps she also stayed on because she and my father were attracted to each other. Soon she was sent to Switzerland to finishing school where she learnt to cook and paint. She was engaged to my father when they both returned to Burma in about 1933, my father cutting short his university study because his father couldn't afford to keep supporting him in England. That's what happens when you have nineteen children! It was my father's first big disappointment not to be able to finish his mining engineering degree, and he always said when we were young that he wanted all of his six children to have a tertiary education even if he and my mother only had rice and salt to eat. And we all did go to university.

My father started working as an apprentice in the Bawdwin silver mines in a town called Namtu, not very far from Hsipaw. But he had to sign a contract stating that he would not get married for three years. He wanted to marry my mother, so he broke his contract. His father could not send him back to England to continue with his degree, and he tried to get an apprenticeship in other mines but he was turned down, so he was facing financial hardship. He decided to go to Mogok, in a mountainous area of the northern Shan states, to a region known as 'the ruby lands', to work in the mines. On the way, he drove his car over a cliff into a deep ravine and was saved by a mine owner. My father boasted ever after that he was admitted to a maternity ward because there were no other facilities, and received eight stitches to his head.

In any case, he survived and my parents were married in 1934. The wedding was a grand and fabulous affair, described by my aunts as 'Burma's wedding of the century'.

The births of my father's first two children followed close on the heels of the marriage. In 1935, a healthy son, Tony, arrived to fulfil the Burmese dream of a son as the first-born, and all the family doted on him. There followed a daughter, myself, in 1936, which must also have pleased my father, although he was not a man to show much emotion.

I'm not sure what income my parents had during this period, but in 1938 when my mother was expecting their third child, Bunny, my father was appointed as an administrator for Kengtung state, so the family moved there. My aunt-in-law, Sao Kyar Nyunt, the wife of his eldest brother who'd been assassinated in 1937, objected to the appointment. She said that if my father were to act as an administrator, her son would not become a chief, so she appealed to the resident representing the

British Government, Captain Robert, to withdraw my father's appointment.

So in 1938, just 45 days after his third child Bunny was born, my father had to move our family back to Hsipaw without a job to go to. The family managed to get along with some income from the state, and another two children were born, Tim in 1939 and Sydney in 1941.

The following year, during World War II, my father took up his first job as administrator of the town of Nawng Khio, which means green lake, and the surrounding villages. Our youngest brother, Gerry, was born there in 1943 during Allied bombing which was intended to prevent the Japanese forces crossing the Goakhteik bridge, which spanned the magnificent Goakhteik Gorge, to reach the northern Shan states.

For years afterwards, whenever I would ask my mother about Gerry's birth, she would describe it in terms of the bombing, which had a big impact on everyone because it meant our local people couldn't cross into some other states until the bridge was repaired – and it was especially traumatic for my mother as her breast milk at first didn't flow naturally to feed her newborn. I remember my Aunt Pansy, my mother's youngest sister, would soak cotton wool in honey and squeeze it into my tiny brother's mouth for some sustenance. From then on, he was pampered all his life.

Before the bombing occurred, my grandmother and my aunts, Millie and Pansy, had crossed the bridge to visit us from Hsipaw. After the bombing they could not return home. My father had to get workmen to build a timber cottage to accommodate them. Then my father's sister, Sao Bo Sawan, took a jungle track to join us as well. She came with a retinue including one cousin, one nephew called Louis, her cook, a maid and the maid's brother. So my father had another bungalow built for them. My aunt vowed not to return to Kengtung as long as her second-eldest brother, Sao Hpom Li, remained as the chief installed by the Thai king. That same year, 1943, Sao Hpom Li would go into self-exile because it was alleged he was part of a plot that caused the assassination of my father's eldest brother, Sao Kawng Tai. After the war, she did return to Kengtung.

So from 1943 three houses stood on my father's estate and we lived there until we all moved to Hsum Hsai in about 1944, when my father was transferred there to administer the town and surrounding villages. He was considered a strict but fair administrator, and his people loved and respected him.

I don't recall how long we stayed there, but it was during this wartime period when I was about eight years old that I experienced the most frightening event of my life – one that haunts me at times. It's strange that I now live in a place that takes my mind back to that earlier time of danger. I live in Sydney's eastern suburbs, at Mascot, close to the airport and under the flight path. All day I hear the sound of aircraft taking off and touching down just above my head. Having lived here for about fifteen years, I almost don't notice the noise as I go about my household chores. What I do notice is when there is no noise, or when the usual sound changes from what we are accustomed to hearing. At these times, I can't help but imagine myself back in a village in Burma that once suffered bombing by the Allied forces intent on stopping the Japanese from advancing north. The droning sound of small aircraft especially, takes me back to those World War II days. Whenever the bombers approached, all the villagers would run into the trenches nearest to wherever they were, whether in the fields, in the yard or inside our home. One day the Allied planes bombed our village by mistake. They were meant to bomb the railway station, but one bomb was dropped in our front yard.

Let me recreate the scene. The morning begins in the usual way. It's cool in our valley. We have had our breakfast of bread and butter and homemade marmalade, and my mother has started cooking for lunch. The kitchen forms the back part of our house, with a corrugated roof that extends into the back yard and next to it a trench that has been dug. Our house is made of a timber floor with matted bamboo walls, plastered with cow dung and whitewashed with lime. Smoke rises from the chimney above the kitchen's wood-fire stove, and I can hear the maid using a mortar and pestle to pound ginger, chilli, garlic and onion to be used in a curry. There's a tree, without leaves, so it must be summer. Our Dalmatian, Candy, is lying in the sun near the kitchen door, always close to my mother who loves dogs.

Bunny, who's nearly seven, has walked over to our grandmother's house at the other end of the town, about two kilometres away. Sydney has been taken to spend the night at my aunt's place, close by my grandmother's home. Tony, Tim, toddler Gerry, two maids, my mother, my father and I are still about the yard.

Suddenly the drone of aircraft is heard. They always used to appear in twos, and here is a pair now. Dubbed 'buffalo brothers', they make a sound of descent as they swoop down – at first high-pitched and ominous then dropping to a deep-throated bellow – which we liken to the sound of buffaloes.

We all run for our lives – Mum and the cook to the trench nearest the kitchen, which doesn't have any roof protection; Dad, my brothers and I to the trench in the front yard which has a roof made of corrugated iron sheets covered with mud or sand.

We take refuge huddling among the bags of rice, potatoes and peanuts, with drums of peanut oil clinking and baskets of onions and garlic spilling out onto the ground. The door at the end of the trench swings open and bangs shut over and over again from the impact of the planes flying low above us, shuddering as they drop their bombs.

My infant brother Gerry points his finger to the roof six feet above our heads, saying, 'boom, boom,' as the sound of the bombs' explosions hits our eardrums. It's an enormous sound. We feel the earth move and shake through an old piece of carpet under our feet. The sides of the bunker beside and above us seem to be shifting and the oil drums clash and clang. The raid takes perhaps ten minutes, a seemingly endless period of time to live through.

'Whee-ee-ee ... varoom ... varoom.'

Then everything is quiet again. The planes seem to have flown off.

Only then, we straighten up from our crouching position and stretch ourselves. I want my mother. When we emerge from our hiding place there is dust everywhere and we see a huge crater made by the bomb just a few yards from our trench.

Mum is emotional and trembling because her trench didn't have a roof. She had chanted every prayer she knew while she and the cook had watched the planes dropping bombs. We cry and laugh at the same time, recounting what we've all just been through. The tears for what might have been, with all of us separated – my other brothers, grandmother and aunts at the other end of the town, my mum in one place and my father, my three brothers and me in another. The laughter is of relief that our lives have been spared.

I'll take up the next part of this story about how we fared, and our father's brilliant plan to protect us, a little later ... but first I want to complete my story of what kind of man my father was by describing events at the end of his life.

My father passed away as a result of diabetes on 15 April 1995. You could say he had a very sweet tooth and didn't limit his sugar intake.

At the time of his death on Burmese New Year's Eve, he and my mother were living in a small cottage within our compound at Seventh Mile in Rangoon. He was very ill and we took him to hospital at three o'clock in the morning, where he died about five hours later. We brought him home soon afterwards for burial because we Buddhists believe that a person needs to be buried during the same year that his or her death occurs. My father had told us that the heat would kill him that year, and in fact he did die at the beginning of the hot season, just a week before my parents' fiftieth wedding anniversary. I felt a great loss and that I had been responsible for his death in some part because I had been concentrating on their anniversary celebration to come rather than on his health. My mother was devastated because she depended on him in every way.

Dad left two bank accounts – one was his personal account while the other was a joint account. My mother and I went to Lashio from Rangoon to pack up her and my Dad's possessions to bring down to Rangoon. I helped her withdraw the money from the bank in Lashio, and as it was my parents' joint account it wasn't difficult to do. The bank manager knew Mum and Dad very well because Lashio was a small town and everybody knew everybody. In fact Mum didn't even need to go to the bank. I brought the forms to withdraw the funds and close the account for her to fill in and sign at home, before taking them back to the bank and bringing the money back for her. She donated all of the money and four bookcases to the local eye ward of the hospital.

It was a heart-wrenching task to pack up Dad's possessions. He treasured whatever he possessed. He had had the house built with his hard-earned money and could only afford a new home after thirty years of service. By the time of his death, he had sold his Skoda and had been driving a Morris Minor which his nephew had given him. I arranged for a truck, which transported goods from Rangoon to Lashio that was going back to Rangoon empty, to carry Dad's Morris Minor. Also on board were my parents' carpets, mattresses, furniture and boxes.

A month after he had passed away, we invited the monks, the elders of the town and friends to attend a traditional ceremony offering food and alms to the monks and praying for my dad to share merits. At that time, a Chinese carpenter brought over a large amount of money to us, saying it was for having bought a wood lathe and a brick-making machine from Dad which hadn't yet been paid for. He also said that since he was able to do well in his carpentry business with the help of the lathe, he was grateful to my father, so he wouldn't charge Mum for installing a cast iron gate. He could have avoided paying the money he owed to Dad. Mum wouldn't have known. These days many conmen carry out scams; in those days past, people lived on trust and kindness.

Back in Rangoon, Mum wanted to withdraw Dad's money from the bank. Dad did not leave a will. He did not need to. In Burmese Buddhist law, when a husband dies the wife is left all his possessions and when a wife dies the husband receives all her properties and money. However, it was no easy task for Mum to retrieve the money that belonged to Dad. The bank teller she saw started being nasty by asking Mum why her name in her signature was spelt Sao Ohn Nyunt with a 't' at the end of the last word, instead of Sao Ohn Nyun – why was there an extra 't', he wanted to know? Then he asked why she had written Sao instead of Saw. We wrote to the bank telling them that Sao and Saw had the same meaning, and the former spelling was the Shan way of pronouncing while the latter was the Burmese pronunciation and spelling. The bank then demanded that her offspring sign a statement that they would not claim the money deposited in the bank. What I had to do was to write to Bun, Tim and Sydney to sign the statement and send it back. This wasn't difficult to do with Bun and Tim, whereas Sydney was supposed to be untraceable since he had gone underground. But he also managed to send the signed statement via a messenger.

Then the bank went a step further by saying that the statements signed already would have to be signed and witnessed by the Burmese ambassador in the respective Burmese embassies for any of my father's children living outside of Burma. I knew that was not possible for Bun, who left Burma with only a certificate of identity. The Burmese revolutionary government would not issue passports to anybody who went overseas unless they were sent on government-approved missions. Tim was the only person who could have done that. For Sydney it was out of the question.

As a last resort, I recounted this to my uncle-in-law who was an ex-army officer. He instructed me to write a letter of appeal to the finance minister who was also an ex-army officer. I did exactly as I had been told and borrowed my uncle's car and driver to deliver the letter personally at the minister's house. I was refused entry and was told to deliver it at the office at the ministry. The minister must have acted promptly because the bank manager soon summoned Mum to the bank and sent someone down to meet her at the bottom of the elevator. Mum was given VIP treatment. However, the manager did not release an order for my mum to withdraw the money. He said she would hear from him in October. It was still May and I asked the manager why wasn't she allowed to have the money, and he said it was a very large amount. My dad would be turning in his grave if he knew that what he had worked for all his life had been robbed from his widow. Mum would have liked to donate it to the same charitable cause she had already given money to, as old people in Burma do when they are old and feeble. Up until we left for Fiji and even until Mum joined us, nothing was heard from the bank, nor has any word been heard ever since.

In another case, Dad had seven shops along the main road and rented them out to various shop owners. They were in Kengtung and he was living too far away in the northern Shan states to collect the rent every month. I was told his sister who lived in Kengtung had an adopted daughter who collected the rents and spent the money on renovations and alterations. Dad never saw any of it. Then when the military government took over, it nationalised all the businesses and the shops became government-owned shops. One manager after another took office, one even building a house behind the shops. My youngest brother Gerry and I tried to retrieve the properties, to no avail. My mother passed away without having any of the money she would have gained if they'd been restored to her. I tell this story to show how the previous government robbed people of their fortunes.

Dad had an orange orchard across the lake from his father's palace. I believe a member of the ruling Revolutionary Council took it and built a house on it.

Another time Dad was given a huge plot of land and with it a mud brick house. It had timber pillars, used as props for a zinc roof. It's my understanding that Dad's sister, Sao Bo Sawan, gave one quarter of the plot to her maid, or adopted daughter. The adopted daughter's older sister wanted a plot too. So another quarter is understood to have been given to her. Another maid wanted the third quarter and I believe my aunt sold it to her, leaving the house with its kitchen cut off from the main part of the house and no land left around it. Dad's brothers were building a cinema hall somewhere near the house and they needed a wider road leading to the hall. So the road was widened by slicing off the front part of the house, leaving it with only three steps leading up to the front door. I've wondered how they could have done this to a brother who was less fortunate than they were and who had to earn his living as a government employee, with a wife and six children to support and to educate.

My father had wanted to write the family history but he said he did not want to hurt anybody. He did start to write it before he passed away. My oldest brother Tony also said he wanted to write our family story and he also died. My youngest brother Gerry would tease my Aunty Millie, asking why she didn't write the family history since she knew the past, the present, and everything she needed to know. She said she didn't want to die yet. Now the task has fallen into my lap and I've been thinking I would like to finish writing before I die, although I too do not want to hurt anybody. Truth is like an onion with many hidden layers.

Family shot taken in 1947, with Khemawadee centre stage

Chapter 4

My parents' wedding

Sao Khun Mong and Sao Ohn Nyunt wed in 1934

As I said, it was a love match. Dad was my mother's choice. She was saved from the ordeal of being given in marriage to another chief who might have had a dozen lesser wives.

Her adoptive father, who was her uncle, made a point not to give her away to another chief. By contrast, he had made the older girls vow not to marry anyone not approved by him, asking them to kneel in front of the altar as they made the vow. By the time my mother was old enough to marry, he was ageing and didn't have any time to arrange a marriage for her, so she was left comparatively free to choose.

One of her cousins, Sao Kyar Nyunt, who was already married to my father's eldest brother, the chief of Kengtung, frowned upon the liaison between my father and mother before their marriage. She would say that a crow had fallen among seagulls, meaning my mother's skin was dark whereas the people of Kengtung were light-skinned, considered superior. My mother's eldest sister also did not approve of the tie at all. For a petite person, my mother was full of strength and courage. After marriage, she would stand by my father through thick and thin, war and peace.

My aunt Sao Thu Nandar, the Mahadevi of Hsipaw, relented and she and her husband, the chief of Hsipaw state, Sao Ohn Kyar, planned my parents' wedding and spent 50,000 rupees for it to be a success. It was considered a fortune in those days, and my parents said they would rather have had the money than the 'splash' my aunt made, considering my father was jobless at the time.

The wedding was held in our native town, Hsipaw, as it was customary for weddings to take place at the bride's home town. It was an elaborate affair. Hundreds of guests attended the wedding ceremony: dignitaries and relatives from Kengtung, the eastern Shan state, and Hsipaw, the northern Shan state, as well as chiefs from most of the other thirty-two Shan states.

The official ceremony took place on 20 April 1934. The marital rites were performed by my mother's brother-in-law, Sao Ohn Kyar, who was the then chief of Hsipaw state, with the help of four Brahmins from Mandalay. The chief tied the knot over the couple's hands with a gold chain over which blessed water was poured from a solid golden bowl, while the Brahmin priests chanted prayers to wish the bridal pair a long and prosperous married life.

The two matrons of honour were older relatives, and the eight bridesmaids included my younger aunts, Millie and Pansy. The two best men were my father's younger brothers, Sao Sai Mong and Sao Khun Suik. So it was quite a large wedding party.

There were thirty-two principalities that made up the federated Shan states, each of which was ruled autonomously by a prince, so accommodation was at a premium. As the Hsipaw chief and his wife, my mother's oldest sister, were the host and hostess of the ceremony, some of my parents' friends stayed in their home and in some in bamboo huts which were built to accommodate them, with the necessities for their comfort provided.

The celebration was held at a picturesque place called Sakhantha, meaning 'pleasant resort'. It was a scenic village where my aunt, the Mahadevi, had her summer palace on a hillock overlooking a lake. In the early morning, the pre-marriage hair-washing ceremony for the bride and groom, symbolic of cleansing away both dirt and evil, was held in a temporary and decorative bamboo hut made of thatch beside the lake.

Then the groom proceeded to the huge ceremonial marquee on an elephant driven by a *mahout*, with my mother and two maids of honour riding in an open car behind and the rest of the retinue following on. The marquee was decorated with orange blossom in accordance with the bride's wishes.

One of the items in the program was a group dance performed by the hostess's maids and there was a stage show with a special dance troupe brought over from Mandalay. To complete the ceremony, there was a seven-foot-high wedding cake with icing well-wishes written in English, at a time when this type of cake was not a traditional Shan or Burmese wedding custom. My mother's family took pride in being among the most cultured, in that it had connections with the Burmese court, patterning its everyday life in accordance with the Burmese royal family. My mother's family had been westernised in many ways, such as in sending their sons to England to be educated and their daughters to finishing schools in Switzerland.

I was told that the total cost of the celebration was unmentionable at that time. When the wedding was over, my father and mother were left with fifty rupees between them, and my father was jobless. Of course, in those days fifty rupees went further than today!

Although this was the first sign of hardship for my parents, they received an enormous number of presents, including two elephants, who it was said later died due to homesickness.

In the olden days, newly married couples couldn't possibly sell any of their excess presents for sentimental reasons and what would have been considered want of dignity. This is in stark contrast to nowadays, even as far back as twenty-five years ago, when newlyweds sell off presents that are less useful to them or if they have too many of the same gift. So my parents learned to cope with presents instead of money, which would have been more useful to them.

I recall as a child being very interested in my parents' wedding. They had a queen-sized bed which I remember was always properly made with a quilted bedcover. At the foot of the bed stood a camphor chest into which, when we children were young, my brother Tim and I would peek. There were our mother's wedding outfit and a leftover roll of silver brocade, which was made into my wedding *htamein*, or *longyi*. Also found there were two huge wedding albums of photographs, well-preserved through almost twenty years of humid monsoon seasons and harsh war-torn conditions. We loved to lift the albums out reverently and look through them slowly, page by page.

On the first page was the photo of the procession led by my father on the decorated elephant, making its way to the temporary bamboo marquee where the hair-washing ceremony was held. We knew the ceremony was only symbolic. The shampoo used consisted of soap acacia, a slimy, frothy hard-cored fruit, and another roasted bean-like fruit belonging to the mimosa family, some hard limes or lemons, and the crushed slippery bark of a tree, all mixed together. This concoction was our traditional shampoo used every few days on the hair and always for special occasions, ranging from the name-giving ceremony to the washing hair ceremony on Burmese Buddhist New Year's Eve.

We also saw the photos taken after the ceremony as the procession made its way back to where the wedding was solemnised, in a huge marquee decorated with garlands of orange blossom and woven bamboo lattice.

My parents had asked a notable Japanese photographer to attend, which would account for the excellent photographs still in good shape to this day. As children we found it amusing to note the connection in sound between his name, Tanaka, and *thanaka*, the bark of the tree we used for make-up. Of course it meant nothing, really. The matter of real interest was that the photographer happened to be a spy and turned up a few years later as a high-ranking officer during the Japanese occupation of Burma.

Indian Brahmin priests officiated at my parents' marriage ceremony

Chapter 5

Escape

Shan hill country

Returning now to my life as a child aged about seven during the war years, there I was, having just survived the bombing of our family compound in the village of Hsum Hsai. Even as a child I understood that our family needed to take refuge by going into hiding.

Within a day or two after the bombing, Dad and his assistants decided to take the whole town into a deep jungle where bamboo huts were built around some caves. We slept in the huts and ran into the caves when aeroplanes approached. It was here that I had my earliest education, not only in both the Burmese and English languages, but also in how to survive under the harshest of conditions. Whenever we heard the sound of the bombers, the elders didn't need to direct us; we kids just raced for shelter in the caves. One day I hid in a hole inside one cave and stayed there while everyone called my name, not trusting to come out until I was sure the bombers had gone.

Someone must have spied on us and reported our whereabouts to the Japanese troops, because one day three officers came to look for Dad, shouting, 'Kankucho! kucho!'[2] I didn't know the meaning of the words at the time but the sound still echoes in my mind. The troops took my father and his bodyguard away on a bullock cart.

Later we heard that my mother's cousin, Sao Kyar Zone, known as Harold, was appointed chief of Hsipaw by the Japanese occupation administration after he hounded my father, with Japanese officers spying on our family before taking him captive. Harold wanted my father's head because my father was a threat to him remaining as chief of the Hsipaw state once the Japanese occupation was over. Harold's cousin, the previous chief, Sao On Kya, had died in 1938, and the chief's post was left unfilled during the British administration leading up to the outbreak of war. After the war, my father was appointed administrator until, in 1947, the Shan state Council elected Harold's younger brother, Sao Kya Seng, known as Charlie, as Hsipaw chief because the people wanted a Hsipaw native, rather than my father who was from Kengtung.

When my father was taken away by the Japanese soldiers, his bodyguard gave them 'Shamashu', a country brew, until they were dead drunk. My father and his bodyguard slipped away, walking at night back through the jungle to the caves. They harnessed bullocks we had with us at the caves' site, and loaded them with bare necessities. Some carts had mattresses laid on them so that my brothers and I were able to sleep as our family group left the site at about 3 am and made its way further through the jungle, reaching some remote villages by sunset. To my brothers and me it felt like a cart race, and during the day we'd often laugh, clap and cheer on the drivers.

The bullocks had their hooves wrapped in torn blankets to make less noise. We travelled for some miles until we reached a village at sunset where the head man served us dinner, consisting of rice and boiled mustard leaves. My brothers started to cry, asking for some cooked meat, so our nannies fed us rice with jaggery (palm sugar). We proceeded on our journey to a place called Kalakwai. The head of the village welcomed all of us – our parents, our aunts, grandmother and their retinue of nannies, as well as a cook who had been with us for years and who had seen all of us being born. The women and children were housed on the upper level of a school building and the ground level was assigned to my father and the men. I don't know how long we were there. At some point we went to another village where there were Allied soldiers with food that had been parachuted in, such as biscuits, cheese, condensed milk in tubes, and tin provisions such as bully beef and sardines. I can remember a Kachin we called 'Uncle Zau Gaung' who remained a friend our family after the war in Lashio, and another fellow in uniform, an Anglo-Indian or Anglo-Burmese, whom we knew as

'Uncle Jacko'. We tucked into the food, eating whatever was given to us. We didn't run out of food while we were there. We each had plain cakes baked in empty kerosene tins, rice cakes made from steamed glutinous rice, black glutinous rice, salt and roasted round sesame seeds. The seeds were pounded using a huge wooden mortar and pestle, and, with glutinous rice, flattened into a slab on a bamboo tray covered in banana leaves. This was our favourite food. We would cut it into slices and eat it while it was still fresh and hot, after being roasted along bamboo skewers over a wood fire. Then we'd peel off the crusts and roast the slices again. When it turned hard it was cut up into cubes and deep fried.

Then the time came for us to go home. The war was over and we had a convoy of bullock carts lined up, ready to start the journey back to Hsum Hsai. My father was greeted by the village people and the townspeople, who were laughing and crying at the same time. Some thought they had been abandoned by him. He was welcomed with music played by a band of village revellers. Then he was served a lunch of rice and meat curry with condiments and vegetables, with the rice presented in a potty they had looted from an empty house, not understanding its purpose as a receptacle for human waste.

We were in Hsum Hsai for some time, until my father was appointed administrator for the Hsipaw state in 1947. The reason my father was appointed was that the chief Sao Ohn Kyar had died in 1938 and had left no heir, yet he was fond of my father and had wanted to speak with him on his deathbed, possibly about taking over the chief's position, and the British government respected my father's administrative abilities. My uncle Charlie finally took up the chief's position later in 1947.

So we all moved to the palace in Hsipaw, which had been designed and built according to my aunt's plan. It was a huge mansion, so huge that six of us and our parents could occupy only half of it. However, the advantage was that there was plenty of space for us to run about, play hide and seek and slide down the staircase banisters.

The grounds were enormous. As you drove through the gates you saw an embankment along the left hand side that resembled a fort, and on the right hand side of the driveway the mansion. There were three steps leading up to the porch. A vast lawn separated the mansion from the summer house, which was a round house with a spiral staircase used to reach the upper level. Not far away there was a tower which housed Burmese musical instruments – a xylophone, a Burmese-style oboe, and a circle of small drums placed in such a way that a player could get into the centre of the circle and flexibly tap the drums with the tips of his fingers. The players were assigned to play a set piece of music at 6 am, 12 pm and 6 pm to remind the townsfolk what time it was. It was a pleasant piece of classical Burmese music, and after the war a recorded version was used to begin the Burmese broadcasting program every morning.

Beyond the summer house was the Dokhtawadi River, a tributary of the Irrawaddy. It was quite shallow and clear, and we could swim in it near the river bank, but it was treacherous during the rainy season due to strong currents. There was a little house of timber and bamboo, with a thatched roof, where one of my grandfather Sir Sao Khe's forty-five ex-wives lived. She would dress in a dark brown robe and her head was shaved. It was known that when he wanted to get rid of a wife he would ask her to donate her hair, which meant that she had her head shaved and became a hermit or a nun. This particular wife chose to become a hermit. We visited her often. She said she was my mum's nursing mother when my mother was adopted by her uncle, the chief. So many interconnections, we Shans have.

I get carried away in these memories – so we might go back to a description of the estate. As I said, on the left hand side of the driveway there was a fort, and an opening through which we would run in and out in games. There was also a big pond made by a bomb which had filled with rainwater. We would play with a rowboat and row around and around in the shallow pond. I forget what the rest of the estate was like. However, we had a wonderful time when we were young there.

Then it was time for us to leave that mansion. The people of the state, prompted by the older relatives of the late chief, demonstrated that they wanted a Hsipaw person to rule them instead of my father, who was a Kentung prince and not a native as he had only married the Hsipaw princess. There was a meeting of the Shan chiefs who gathered at the Hsipaw haw, or palace, which was spacious enough to accommodate them all, about twenty chiefs with their bodyguards. Some stayed in the summer house; some had tents set up on the lawns. My brother and I were at boarding schools, but our youngest brother was still too young to be sent away, so he saw it all.

This was the meeting that decided my grandfather's youngest brother Sao Oh, who was Charlie and Harold's father, could not be the chief even though he was the uncle of the late chief, because Sao Oh had not been a good ruler when appointed earlier. So Charlie became chief and my father had to settle for handing over the administrator's job.

Dad had been hurt twice, once in Kengtung when the British government resident, Captain Robert, had overruled his appointment, and now in Hsipaw. So he left Hsipaw to join the frontier services and worked in Bhamo in the Kachin state near the Chinese border, where he set up the mechanical plant division for the Shan public works department. Later he moved it to Lashio, the capital of the northern Shan states. He preferred being stationed there instead of Taunggyi, the capital of the southern Shan states, where the high-ranking officials had their headquarters.

My father loved being independently placed. He was in charge of the heavy equipment and an office which housed him and his assistant and an engineer. There were foremen, drivers and fitters, and another assistant engineer was placed in the Taunggyi public works department. My father worked for the Shan state government as an executive engineer, supporting a wife and six children whom he educated. He brought us up strictly. He was a straightforward person and a good Buddhist. He was always protective towards my mother, who adored him.

We children in boarding school never went back to Hsipaw during those years, instead going to Lashio for our next holiday break. I remember attending the monastery every full moon day. All of us would dress up in traditional clothes and take some rice, candles, tea leaves and flowers to pay respect. We would listen to the sermons, say our prayers and share merits with the living and the dead, as well as spiritual and celestial beings. Spiritual beings are considered by the Burmese to be those spirits surrounding humans, while celestial beings live in the heavens above.

My father travelled a lot, all over the Shan states while he was stationed in the northern Shan state. He would take us to his birthplace, Kengtung, situated in a lush valley, every year during our summer holidays while he carried out inspections of the heavy equipment and the road repairs and maintenance needed. Two legends associated with the valley concern a golden deer and a beautiful bird, indicating how picturesque the area was considered. We would rest in the inspection bungalows at night. They were equipped with beds, a table and chairs, and pots, pans and crockery. The keeper of the bungalow would provide us with water and firewood. My father had a boxful of tea, coffee, condensed milk and dried and fried food to last us four days until we reached Kengtung. Usually we arrived at a bungalow before dark. The hot water would be ready and we would have tea and biscuits. Then later we would have a dip in a pond from water supplied by a spring further up the hill which flowed down a set of bamboo pipes. Usually the bathing spots were located in a secluded and bushy place, but in full view of the travellers in the bungalows which were conveniently built on a hillock. We had our sarongs wrapped around us so there was no concern about bathing out in the open in the shallows. Nor did the village girls show any concern, pulling off their sarongs to swim naked as soon as they immersed themselves in the deep water.

After dinner we would lie down and soon we would be fast asleep after the exertion of the day. We would wake up fully rested, having slept on camp cots, using our canvas bedrolls and pillows that we'd carried with us. We'd have breakfast, usually of fried rice, and were ready to continue on to Kentung.

The Shans and Burmese are a superstitious people and my father was quite superstitious. He wouldn't travel on the 13th day of the lunar month nor travel with a total of nine persons in a car. It is believed that there exists a spirit governing nine of the Shan states and you need to avoid offending the spirit by travelling. The unluckiest day according to the Myanmar calendar falls when the number representing a day of the week and the actual full date adds up to the number 13.

Dad was provided with a Land Rover with room for five siblings, a nanny, my parents and a driver – a total of nine. Once when we were travelling through a teak forest, the car's axle broke. The truck that travelled behind us had all the equipment for repairs, including welding machines. It took the workers until dusk to set it right, and we stopped at a place called Kun Hing, a village with a bungalow where we could sleep comfortably overnight. We drove to the river's edge the next morning. Again the axle broke.

After the second incident, my dad asked the driver to travel in the truck behind to dispel the bad luck. We were able to cross the Ta Kaw River on a bamboo ferry which carried the Land Rover with eight of us aboard instead of nine. The truck followed on the next trip down the river to the town, Mong Ping, where we spent the night.

Finally, after travelling up hill and down dale, we arrived at our destination, my father's birthplace which was my grandfather's principality, Kengtung. My grandfather had passed away by then but my father was very pleased to be back in that region even though he'd vowed never to return.

Chapter 6

My forefathers

Uncle Sao Kawn Tai and great-grandfathers Sao Khun Hseng and Sao Kawn Kiao Intaleng

The founder of Chiang Mai, King Mangrai, is said to have conquered the Was in 1243 AD, in the area where Kengtung, also known as Khemarat, the eastern Shan state, now exists. There followed a succession of chiefs until the dynasty came to a tragic end when my father's nephew, Sao Sai Long, the 40th chief, was reportedly forced to surrender his autonomy to the Burmese military government in 1959. He was my cousin, related to me as the son of my father's brother who married my mother's sister. His surrender had followed a difficult period of civilian rule during which time the Burmese resistance leader, General Aung San, was assassinated in July 1947. Killed along with him were eight men, including a chief of the Shan states, Sao Sam Htun, whose son I would later marry.

Some consider that the British were behind the assassinations or that someone not convicted was the instigator.[3] However, the justice system in Burma convicted the political leader, Galon U Saw, as conspiring to plan and carry out the assassination with others who were also convicted.

Six months after the assassinations, in January 1948, Burma and the Shan states gained independence from the British. The nationalist leader, U Nu, was elected prime minister and a parliament was established with representation given to the Shan states and other minority states, with their chiefs holding some portfolios. The Yawng Hwe Shan chief, Sao Shwe Thaike, was elected by the parliament to be the first president of Burma.

A sum was given to each of the chiefs in compensation for losing their independent status upon joining the national government, calculated according to the yearly revenue they received. All thirty-three chiefs of the federated Shan states were obliged to sign an agreement on 24 April 1959 to hand over their hereditary rights and administrative powers.[4]

It is sad that the dynasty had to come to an end in this way. The thirty-three Shan chiefs were given just twenty-five seats in the chamber of nationalities. However, it was not for long, because they were rounded up on 2 March 1962 when they all came down to the capital, Rangoon, for the parliamentary session. Most were incarcerated in the Insein Annex prison for five years, and some for six or seven years.

My youngest uncle, public works minister for the Shan states Sao Yawt Mong, came home after seven years. The last chief of Kengtung, Sao Sai Long, had been in hospital recovering from an appendix operation when the coup struck and he was carried off on a stretcher to prison. He was released after six years in custody, and though still young, he was wealthy enough not to need to work. He had ruled the largest principality and was therefore the richest chief. I remember him as being active and having a sense of humour. He would tease the older chiefs and his uncles and aunts. Our whole clan respected, even loved, him and we were very sad when he passed away in 1997. He would have had a great funeral if he hadn't been forced to relinquish his powers, but although he was given a traditional funeral, most of his relatives were overseas by the time he died. His demise signified the end of a great kingdom, and the earlier demolition of his palace, with all its pomp and glamour, was an achievement that many envious Burmese had always craved.

For, you see, although we Shans think of ourselves as Burmese, we always call ourselves 'Shan'. As a Shan, I've come to understand that if we have the word 'Sao' in front of our name, which denotes that we are from a ruling family, and the word 'Shan' after our name, stating our nationality, which is compulsory on forms, it means it's always hard to find a job due to discrimination. For instance, when my brother went for a job with the Burmese public service in the 1960s, he was told that as he was a Shan he didn't need a job and could go underground. Another example was when my brother-in-law applied for a position in the foreign service and was turned down ostensibly because the rules about who would be permitted to be appointed had been laid down by his uncle, a former foreign minister, who was a political prisoner at that time. The country is now called Myanmar, its original formal written name, revived recently, since the British had used only the colloquial name Burma during their rule. But will the new name wash away age-old prejudice? We can only pray for such liberation.

So the rule of the Shan chiefs came to an end in 1997, and with it the exchange of sisters and daughters for the sake of alliances, the presentations of daughters to the Burmese kings for the protection of their states, and the holding of sons of chiefs at the Burmese king's palace not only for education but mostly as hostages in order to have the chiefs abstain from rebellions against the Burmese king. The king himself was taken captive by the British in 1885 and held in a palace in Ratnagiri, overlooking the sea, on the west coast of India, together with his queen and retinue. As people say these days, 'what goes around comes around'.

It's sad to think that the fate of many Shan chiefs' daughters and sisters was also not favourable. A Burmese military administration took power in the Shan states on 1 December 1952, said to have been necessary due to 'unstable conditions'.[5]

I was studying for my matriculation examination at the time and heard about the administration but was not aware of the changes that it brought. Only a few years ago, I came to realise the fates determined for one after another of the Shan princesses, and also those of ordinary Shan girls who were pretty. Many were snatched up into marriage by Burmese military officers, little knowing that General Ne Win had a scheme to not only rule the Shan states but also to wipe out its genetic heritage by encouraging his men to marry Shan women. I try to reconcile myself to the idea that in the days of the chiefs, the Shan ladies enjoyed living in the court simply for the sake of prestige and protection. Since the chiefs were replaced by the army officers, the girls would rather be married to them. Some were educated and would become averse to arranged marriages and in favour of women's rights. I know my father would not have liked me to be given away to a chief to be just one wife among many, nor would he have persuaded me to marry an army officer, although he would mingle with them and play golf with them.

As for myself, I was busy studying and I had my own choice of a boyfriend, whom I married. I would not like to share him with anybody else even if he could afford to keep many wives. As it happened, he was an orphaned chief just struggling with his tutor's pay, then he became an advocate paid only when he had a case, and later a member of parliament for two years.

After that, my husband was placed under detention for five years, during which time his bank account was frozen. What could I do but find a job and work for twenty years? And even after that period of time, I was ineligible for a pension because there'd been a break in my employment. By no means could Hom have taken on another wife.

My paternal grandfather

Sao Kawn Kiao Intaleng, my father's father, was born in 1873 and by heredity became the chief of the principality of Kengtung in the eastern Shan states. He received his order of appointment as Sao Pha, or chief, from the British government.

This is how it happened. My grandfather's father, Sao Kawng Tai, was the 38th chief of Kengtung state, born in 1829 and coming to power in 1880. He was succeeded by his son, a brother to my grandfather, Sao Kawng Hkam Hpu, the 39th chief, in 1886.

Before he became the 40th chief, my grandfather was a gold trader when he married my grandmother, Sao Nang Phong. It was during one of his gold trading trips, homeward bound, that he stopped to have lunch. To his amazement, as soon as he opened his lunch box he saw maggots in it. He closed the lid, declaring it was a sign of good luck – an omen. As he continued his journey home, he saw a group of people coming towards him bringing with them a festive air – playing the long drum, the short drum, a set of gongs and the cymbals. My grandfather asked them what was going on. They said that his brother had passed away and they had come to welcome him as the new chief.

My grandfather was a good Buddhist. He abolished slavery in Kengtung state and for that he was given the title of KSM, a gold chain of honour awarded by the British government for exceptionally distinguished service to the state. He was also invited to attend the Coronation Durbar for Edward VII held in Delhi in 1903. As the chief of Kengtung he was present at a visit by King George V to Rangoon in 1905. Again, he was invited to attend another Imperial Durbur held in Delhi in 1911, when King George and Queen Mary were presented to an assembly of dignitaries and princes as the Emperor and Empress of India . Sao Kawn Kiao Intaleng was also granted an award for services during World War I. His travel to India inspired him to have the Kengtung chief's palace, or haw, built in the style of the palaces of the Indian maharajas. He also visited Ceylon and the Straits Settlements.

I remember my father relating to me how when his father travelled from Burma to India by ship, he disembarked on an elephant which was decorated in silver regalia. When he saw the maharajah's elephants decorated with gold regalia, he ordered his retinue to take the elephant back to the ship. He said he'd rather walk.

My grandfather had six wives and twenty-one offspring. After he was installed as chief, he married another chief's daughter and made her the principal wife, or Mahadevi, so my grandmother was demoted to wife number 2. There followed wives numbers 3, 4, 5 and 6. Wife number 6 – the youngest and the favourite – was my grandmother's niece, which was heartbreaking for my grandmother. To add to her grief, my grandfather had a mansion built for each wife except my grandmother, who was asked to live with his mother. My grandmother died young, leaving six children, which was proof of her broken heart, according to her daughter, my aunt Sao Bo Sawan. The youngest of my grandmother's children had had to share love and milk with wife number 5's son and daughter. My father shared milk with wife number 3's eldest daughter and they became very close as they grew up together. All the children had respect for each other and their stepmothers, who also showed respect for each other. I remember visiting Kengtung one summer holiday when I was about fifteen and my aunt would go downtown to sit, smoke and chat with the stepmothers every day. Then after lunch they would gather at my aunt's residence to play cards. On Sabbath days Uncle Khun Suik, or Uncle Denis, would drive around in an open jeep and wake everyone up at 5 am to get ready to go to the monastery to pray. It was a gathering of the clan. Another place where the clan converged was the lake behind my aunt's residence. The annual boat racing took place there with my uncle an event judge, and I can remember even in the 1950s the clan gathering to watch the boat racing. Uncle Khun Suik would sit in his own motor boat with a starter's gun in his hand and a whistle in his mouth.

My maternal grandfather

Very little is known about my mother's father, Sao Lu, who was the younger brother of Sir Sao Hke, the chief of Hsipaw state. He had five wives and came from the Ohn Pawng dynasty in the northern Shan states.

Hsipaw is the name of the principality as well as the main town where the chiefs of the dynasty resided. Situated about seventy kilometres from Lashio, the capital of the northern Shan states, it was ruled by a succession of Ohn Pawng kings, stretching back even before the life of my great great grandfather, Sao Khun Kya Htun, in the mid-19th century. I believe he was a general during the reign of the Ohn Pawng Maharaja, Sao Khun Paw, and King Mindon, the second last King of Burma, who reigned in Amarapura near Mandalay from 1853 to 1878 and held dominion over the Ohn Pawng chiefdom.

After one particular conflict had ended, it's said that King Mindon did not allow my great great grandfather Sao Khun Kyar Htun to return to Ohn Pawng, instead keeping him in his palace, educating and taking good care of him.

But the people of Ohn Pawng asked for his return as their ruler. Sao Khun Kyar Htun told King Mindon Min that he would allow his son Sao Hkun Kyar Khaing, my great grandfather, to remain for King Mindon to bring him up as his own son. So King Mindon is believed to have been satisfied with the arrangement. A daughter, Nang Hseng Kye Tha, was also sent from Ong Pawng and given the status of a queen.

On his father's death, my great grandfather, who had changed his name to Sao Khun Hseng, became the chief. But King Thibaw of Mandalay is reported to have disliked him and sent him to Rangoon.

Later Sao Khun Hseng is chronicled as having had a difficult career as a jewel merchant. It's understood that in 1882 in Rangoon, he shot two of his servants under the impression that they were plotting to take his life, and he was tried and sentenced to death. This was commuted to transportation but after a period he was released and expelled from the British territory, going to live in Karenni state. About four years later, after the British troops took Mandalay, my great grandfather Khun Hseng raised an army to rule in Hsipaw again. He then became the first Shan chief to submit to the British government.

I have often wondered whether, with this great history of his forebears behind him, my grandfather Sao Lu, the son of Khun Hseng, ever felt he could not have lived up to the task of even nominal chiefdom.

As a boy, my grandfather Sao Lu was taken captive with two of his brothers by King Thibaw and held in his Mandalay palace. The king is reported to have said that he wanted to get rid of 'the reeds' by pulling them out, roots and all – in other words, to have them killed. But they were protected and taken to live in a village, and finally they were saved when the British took over Burma.[6]

It was a relief to his family, as it was generally believed that King Thibaw's wife was responsible for the deaths of any number of relatives who might have threatened the throne, having them secured in velvet sacks and trampled by elephants so that 'royal blood' would not spill on the ground, as legend has it.

After his release Grandfather Sao Lu would have been educated in the manner of royal Shan sons, learning to ride, hunt, wield a sword, shoot with bow and arrows, and follow other court customs.

After finishing school, my grandfather was sent to Mandalay in central Burma to attend a police training school, as it was also considered a prerequisite for the chief and his sons to undergo training of that sort. While he was there, he heard of a certain rich man's daughter by the name of Khin Padauk. Her beauty was known far and wide, and my grandfather became infatuated with her.

I don't remember anyone telling me about how he courted her, but it was known that he had driven an elephant next to her window and taken her away to the Shan states by train. She had been in the Shan states since she was about sixteen years of age and had learnt to speak Shan. We've never heard anything of her family, and even laugh about the possibility that they might have disowned her. When I was growing up there, we only knew two of her relatives, both grandsons of my grandmother's brother or sister. The older man worked as a clerk for my father and the younger man grew up with my younger aunts.

According to my grandmother, Grandfather Sao Lu was sent to England to study agriculture, and on his return to Lashio he began to build an irrigation system by digging some trenches. But someone reported this to his brother, the chief, telling him that Sao Lu was plotting to dethrone him by making excavations for military purposes. So the chief, Sao Khe, ordered his younger brother to tour the rest of the Shan states. When he returned home he called out to his wife, my grandmother Khin Padauk, 'Dauk, oh dearest Dauk, I've brought back four chief's daughters as wives for you to be served.' It was fortunate for my grandmother that they all lived in harmony and none of the other wives produced any offspring.

Sadly, my grandmother was widowed when my mother's eldest sister, the firstborn daughter, was about nine years old. At that time my mother and her sister, Sao Thu Nandar, were adopted by their uncle, Sir Sao Khe, the chief of Hsipaw.

Before my grandfather Sao Lu died, he invited to his death bed the advisor to the chief, Mg Mg Ba, who was his schoolmate from his police school days in Mandalay. He requested Mg Mg Ba to take care of my grandmother, Khin Padauk, who was still young and beautiful. He said that if his older brother took her as his wife, she would become wife number 42, whereas should Mg Mg Ba marry her, she would only be wife number 2. She did marry Mg Mg Ba and had two more daughters with him. They were my favourite aunties – Aunty Millie and Aunty Pansy.

Sao Lu had had five wives and only two daughters to carry on his lineage, and, as I said, even they were officially adopted by his older brother, the chief Sir Sao Khe. The chief loved my mother as a true daughter. He only had one son, Sao Ohn Kyar, born in 1893, who was a cousin but also an older adoptive brother to my mother. My mother adored him, and he took care of her, teaching her ballroom dancing and how to ride horses, as well as sending her to finishing school in Switzerland. He married my mother's older sister, his stepsister. Later he performed my mother and father's marriage ceremony and my mother even believed that her son Tim was a reincarnation of him.

Even though my mother's adoptive father, the chief Sir Sao Khe, was able to have his final total of 45 wives live comfortably, he became bankrupt after studying alchemy, so some of the wives had to sell their possessions – such as fur coats – to my grandmother, who was well provided for while her second husband was alive.

It's said that my grandfather, Sir Sao Khe, succeeded in his alchemy studies and after death was elevated to the hierarchy of spiritual beings, and still looks after his descendants to this day.

Sir Sao Khe *Ceremony dress*

Chapter 7

My husband

The marriage book offered to the monks as a meritorious deed after a wedding

My husband's name is Sao Hso Hom. He is a Tuesday-born. I mention the day of his birth because we in Burma give our children names dependent on the day of the week on which a baby is born. Hsa is one of five Burmese alphabets which comes in a group of alphabets used for Tuesday-borns.

Hso means 'tiger'; Hom means 'to rule'. So his name means 'the ruler of the Shans, known as the tiger race'. But as fate would have it, that would not be his destiny.

Hom was born on 19 February 1935. When he was four years old he was sent to a boarding school run by Italian nuns in Kalaw, a town over ninety kilometres from his birthplace, Mong Pawn. His father, Sao Sam Htun, was the chief of Mong Pawn state in the southern Shan states, and his mother was the daughter of Sir Sao Khin Maung, chief of Mong Mit in the northern Shan states. She was given in marriage to the Mong Pawn chief at the age of 17. They had five children. My husband-to-be, Sao Hso Hom, was their second child.

During World War II, Japanese troops occupied Burma. When the Japanese retreated in 1943, Hom's father had to flee with his family to a mountain village called Nar Loong. There his wife and their three younger children were left with guards while he and his eldest daughter, Sao Nandar or Peggy, and his son, Hom, went on to a United States secure forward camp and flew to Bahmo, a town in the Kachin state in the north of Burma. News came of Hom's mother, the Mahadevi, being ill, so the family returned to the mountain village, but by the time they arrived, Hom's mother had died, leaving his father a widower with five children to look after. After the war ended in 1945, Hom's father was chosen by the Shans, Kachins, Chins and Kayahs to be the counsellor to the governor for the frontier areas during the Panglong conference of 1947.

Hom's father represented the frontier areas throughout 1947, when, in a cabinet meeting presided over by General Aung San, both politicians were assassinated, among a group of seven who were killed.[7]

As Hom was now orphaned, he, along with his sister Peggy and his younger brother Sao Kai Hpa, were brought down to Rangoon by an uncle, Sao Hkun Hkio, who was chief of Mong Mit state, head of the Shan states and the Burmese foreign minister. He sent all three children and his own youngest brother to Darjeeling, the boys to attend school at St Joseph's College and Hom's sister to attend Loreto Convent. It was too far away and too expensive for the children to go home for school holidays, so they were placed in the care of British guardians. The guardians couldn't pronounce their names, so Hom, his brother Kai and his Uncle Sao Khun Htun were called Tom, Dick and Harry.

The government of the time would not allow money to be sent abroad so the Darjeeling school fees couldn't be paid beyond two years, and the boys were moved to another school, St Paul's in Rangoon.

In the meantime, my uncle, Sao Sai Mong, and his wife, Daw Mi Mi Khaing, reopened a school that used to be the Shan chief's school, meant for the sons and nephews of the Shan chiefs. With the help of the chiefs and the townspeople, the school was ready to take in students from all over the Shan states. My Aunty Mi Mi Khaing[8] was the principal, an English headmaster was provided by the British Council, and various teachers from the town were recruited. The school was run along the same lines as the missionary schools, with strong discipline, including caning of boys. But instead of teaching Christianity, it taught Buddhism. Hom and his brother were sent there as boarders.

Hom passed his matriculation exam in 1952. His uncle was a politician, a head of state and foreign minister. He travelled a lot and had little time to give Hom parental guidance. Hom was mostly left at home with a cook to feed him regularly, so he read books and learnt English by reading comics. He also played chess with a friend next door. The only outdoor sport he took up was rowing. He rowed in the winning novices team championships at the Rangoon University monsoon regatta in the academic year 1953-54, and the following year his team won the Green Challenge for fours in the annual regatta.

During that time Hom's uncle was undecided about whether Hom should be sent to study in England or just attend Rangoon University. Eventually Hom enrolled himself as an arts faculty student in Rangoon and passed his intermediate examination as an 'outstanding student'. Two years later, in 1956, he obtained a Bachelor of Arts degree. Although he was an honours student, he couldn't wait to work as an English tutor because he wanted to support his youngest sister in a school in Rangoon. The following year he received an English Honours degree and a university gold medal for his achievement. The cost of the gold was subsidised by Hom's uncle as the university could not afford to pay the full cost of the medal.

Hom had already joined the boy scouts; then he joined the university training corps. It was fortunate for him in one way. I think all this training in physical endurance contributed to his being able to withstand the future tough life he had the misfortune to have bestowed upon him.

We married in 1959. It was a big wedding. All the chiefs in the Shan states, the public works division officers in the state, and my father's former and current bosses, were present. It was the custom to stay at the bride's town for one week. After that we were sent off to Hom's state accompanied by our town's elders. There we were welcomed by my groom's elders, and people in general.

Hom's uncle wanted him to be a politician, like himself. So Hom studied law for two years and attained his advocateship. In the meantime, he was appointed chief of Mong Pawn state by the President of Burma, U Win Maung. Mong Pawn state had had no chief since 1947 when Hom's father, Sao Sam Htun, was assassinated. It had been governed by an administrator. In 1958, just over six months before our wedding in May 1959, the army headed by General Ne Win took over the governing of Burma. This led to the Shan chiefs surrendering their powers at gunpoint. As I explained earlier, under duress they were given twenty-five seats in the Chamber of Nationalities and an amount of money as some compensation, according to the revenue they had received from their respective states. These were troubled times.

Our first daughter Seng was born in February 1960. We named her Seng Sirikit, Seng meaning 'jewel', and Sirikit after the Queen of Thailand, as her visit coincided with Seng's birth. She came two weeks early and weighed just five pounds but, to my relief, she was heavy enough to miss out on being placed in an incubator. I'm sure the premature birth was due to the amount of work I did in the lead-up. My aunt Sao Thu Nandar had come down from Hsipaw to Rangoon for a heart operation at the Rangoon general hospital. Aunty Millie also arrived for an operation at the women's hospital. So I spent evenings visiting them in their wards, taking them their meals. Seng was born 7 o'clock on a Tuesday with a doctor and nurse present, and I didn't experience much pain. Hom sent a telegram to my parents and they had rushed down on an overnight train from Lashio to share our happiness.

After a week in hospital, my newborn Seng and I went home to family in Rangoon. Now I understand why my brother Tony was given so much attention as a first-born, because Seng too was surrounded by her grandparents, aunts and relatives. Uncles and their friends took turns holding her tightly wrapped little body in their arms for photographs. It was a wonder that she turned out to be a tough person who won the V championship award for inter-university judo. She could take care of herself.

Years later she would go bicycle riding alone along a lane heading towards the monastery compound. Boys playing football nearby teased her. She just got off the bicycle, unbuckled her belt and started whipping around. There was another time when she was given a love letter. Her reaction was to strike the giver with her folded umbrella. Another incident occurred on a bus when she was aged about eighteen. Buses in Burma were so congested one was lucky to get a standing place. Sometimes passengers would end up facing each other, and there were pickpockets galore. One day Seng was standing on a crowded bus facing a man when he brazenly reached out and grabbed her wallet from her breast pocket. Seng snatched it back with her left hand and at the same time punched the man with her right hand. She was so scared when she realised what she had done that she got off at the next stop and began walking towards a friend's house at great speed. She did not turn around to look back at the man who was swearing at her. And she did not dare go home by herself, so her friend accompanied her home in a three-wheeled taxi.

In 1960 at the age of twenty-five, Hom was elected by the Shan state council to represent the Shan state of Mong Pawn in the Chamber of the Nationalities. He was also a member of the Shan state Legislative Council which held its meetings in Taunggyi, in the southern Shan state. That same year he was chosen by the Chamber of Nationalities to study federal government systems and attend the United Nations Assembly to hear an address to the Assembly by Cuba's leader, Fidel Castro, which lasted six hours.

Hom's uncle, Sao Hkun Hkio, was the head of the Shan state, and Hom's brother Kai served as private assistant to his uncle. At an all-states conference in Taunggyi in 1961, Hom became a member of a constitutional reform committee.

Our second baby was born in January 1962 at the same SDA hospital where Seng had been born. Sao Orawan translates as 'beautiful heart'. But we called her 'Ouie' at home as she was a plump baby. She weighed 6 lbs and would grow to be a chubby little girl with a fringe and two little plaits. But when she was only three months old, her father was taken away to be placed under detention.

On 2 March 1962 there was another coup d'etat when General Ne Win took over through force of arms the rule of the country from the former legally elected parliament. It called itself a 'revolutionary' government. All Shan ministers, members of parliament and the heads of various departments of the Shan states were arrested and placed in detention as 'honoured guests of the government'. The ministers and MPs from all fourteen divisions had come down to Rangoon, the capital at that time, for a parliamentary session. The general had given orders for his officers to round up all the ministers and MPs from the various places where they usually stayed when there was a parliamentary session. A total of forty-three men were taken to Ye Gyi Aing, an improvised interrogation centre where several buildings were secured by barbed wire. Later they were transferred to Insein, Burma's largest correctional prison, where two long, double-storey buildings surrounded by barbed wire had been built to house them.

The political prisoners were assigned to live inside the annexe next to the prison in those two long buildings as well as a building furthest from the main gate which had previously housed criminals sentenced to life imprisonment. Each long building housed twenty-two prisoners. There was a house in between the two buildings where the first Burmese president after the country gained independence, Sao Shwe Thaike (who was also the chief of Yawng Hwe and had become the speaker of the house), was placed on the upper floor to live alone. There were another two specially built small houses where the Burmese foreign minister, Sao Hkun Hkio, who was Hom's uncle and also head of the Shan states, and the chief of the Karreni state, Sao Wunna, were incarcerated for six years. After Hom's uncle was arrested, within seven days his English wife Mabel was ordered to leave Burma for England by the military government.

My father's third-youngest brother who was the police chief for Kengtung state, and my mother's cousin, Sao Kyar Zone, who was Shan state secretary, were also among those imprisoned.

After about a month interrogating the Shan members of parliament and others imprisoned, the military intelligence decided to come for Hom. He knew they would come sooner or later. Two military intelligence officers came in a Volkswagen 'Beetle' which was minus a door. The two approached me and said they had come to take Hom away for questioning, and I told them he was seeing off my aunt at the central station. They replied that they could wait until Hom arrived home. They also said I should pack a bedroll and some clothes and toilet requisites for him. I was so upset I didn't know where to begin. We were so used to travelling that we had a canvas bedroll at hand. So, together with a blanket, a pillow and towel, I packed singlets, shirts, underpants and *longyis* (sarongs worn by Burmese men similar to Indian attire) for Hom to take to prison. I had fried some dried prawns and chillies which I put in an empty jar. Another jar was used for roasted Shan tealeaves. I don't normally get flustered, but I felt very anxious. The officers said Hom would be away for a while. I couldn't have known that 'a while' would mean five years!

Hom was placed in the back seat of the car. He didn't show any emotion as he was led away. He just went along quietly; he didn't even look back, perhaps thinking that he'd be away just a few days.

My elder daughter was aged two years and three months and my younger daughter just three months old when Hom was taken away. They couldn't understand what had happened to their father. Towards evening, friends and relatives had heard about Hom's arrest and came over to visit me and offer some comfort. My sister-in-law came to stay with us, bringing an overnight bag with her. She was single and still studying at the university. Hom's younger brother Kai also came over to stay, and my younger brother Bunny was already staying with us. The next evening John Watson from the Australian embassy and Joan Frank from the British Council library stopped their car at the top of our road and walked down our little lane, carrying a box of tinned provisions and a carton of books on their shoulders so that I could send these to Hom.

In the beginning we were allowed to send food and books. Later on, books were prohibited. *Time* and *Newsweek* magazines were provided for inmates in the gaol. At first the detainees were given breakfast, mid-morning drinks, lunch and dinner. But after a month or so, the government ordered that all prisoners, regardless of whether they were political or criminal, would be treated in the same way, and only two meals were to be dispensed. However, we, the wives of the detainees, were allowed once a fortnight to write letters and send our husbands money (worth about $25 in Burmese currency at that time). We would also give them toilet requisites or whatever small items the prisoners had asked for in letters. My two girls and I would walk to the war office carrying some money, a letter and whatever Hom had asked for in his last letter. With the money that I sent, Hom would ask the lance corporal in charge to buy pork, bananas and vegetables.

Hom learnt how to cook, taught by an older MP who was a vegetarian. The lance corporal would make a list of the food items needed and would go to the market nearest the gaol to buy them. He eventually married the bazaar seller who thought he was rich, being able to buy so much.

Every fortnight when I went to the war office, my girls, Seng and Orawan, would come along. I would say, 'Let's send these letters to Hpa Hpa' (the name meaning father and chief). One day the sergeant who accepted the letters was not there, and

Orawan said, 'Hpa Hpa is not here.' She didn't know who her father was. I felt sick when I realised it.

It was fortunate for us that we'd had built a little brick house in Rangoon, which we were able to live in while Hom was in prison. And I was lucky to have my parents. My father had been offered a manager's post at a company which he had been dealing with while working for the government. His experience had come from buying heavy equipment, such as bulldozers, motor graders and other machinery and accessories for the Shan state public works department. When my father got the manager's job at the Autocars company, my parents moved to Rangoon and were given a huge building, formerly a girls' school, to live in, as well as operate the business from a showroom in front of the building. The whole of the ground floor was empty, so my father asked me if I wanted to move into the large hall there with my two little girls. They were aged five and three by that time. The Methodist school was just a street away, so they were enrolled there for the morning shift.

I had not completed my graduate course when I was married. However, I studied for a Bachelor of Arts degree using my eldest and my first younger brother's books and notes. I sat the exam in March 1965, graduating soon afterwards, and then applied for a tutor's post in December 1965. I needed the qualification for a job as I didn't know how long Hom would be away or whether he would be released at all.

The military government had frozen our bank account, so I couldn't have survived without paid employment. I rented out our little house to an up-and-coming Burmese actor who was one of two best men at our wedding. I was doing quite well going to a teaching job, but I dreaded it. Every day when I woke I would be nervous about how I could stand in front of the class and take on the teacher's role. I was shy, you see. Once when I was asked to give an impromptu talk in front of other teachers, I asked my professor if I could get a zero instead of speaking. He said that he would set me a subject that I knew well, some story about my brothers. But a friend who attended the talk said later that I blushed so much that I looked like a hen trying to lay an egg. As a child, my father had always said to me, 'Louder, Biddy! Louder,' and the family joke was that the first time he said it I'd responded by saying, 'Louder, louder,' thinking he simply wanted me to repeat the word after him. By the time I was an adult and was required to stand in front of a classroom, I still hadn't completely overcome my timid nature.

In the mornings I would walk the children to their school, then go on by bus to the University of Rangoon, where I worked, returning by bus in the afternoon. My parents' lady cook, who was quite sober during the day, would fetch the children home from school at lunchtime. By nightfall she would be drunk. She would cook for our family of nine, the group including my two girls, my parents, my eldest and youngest brothers, and my father's nephew, Desmond, who was robbed of his chieftainship by the military government while he was studying in England.

Desmond was never happy because he was not in custody along with the other chiefs. He felt conflicted: he didn't want people to think that he was either small fry or a sympathiser, yet he would have nightmares about uniformed men coming to arrest him. There was another member of the family residing with us, Reggie, who was waiting for a lawyer's job. He had obtained a law degree in Melbourne – but he was neither fluent in Burmese nor familiar with the Burmese legal system, so it was fortunate that he was later able to join his Australian wife and two children in Stawell, Victoria.

The new Burmese military government had nationalised most of the foreign companies and businesses in Burma. The Autocars company was nationalised and my father couldn't work for the measly pay that the government offered of 126 Kyats per week, or equivalent to $31.50 – the exchange rate in those days being $US1 to K4. However, my father was lucky enough to be offered another manager's post in a Swedish match factory in Mandalay in central Burma. But that meant my little girls and I needed to move house. I had sold the little house we had built before Hom's arrest, so now I bought another in Highland Avenue, just over ten kilometres from the centre of the city. It had two bedrooms, two bathrooms, one sitting/dining room, a pantry which served as a kitchen, and two rooms downstairs for maids. We moved into one bedroom, while two of my brothers and Hom's young half-brother occupied the other bedroom. The girls were now enrolled in another school closer to our new home, as the first school was about eleven kilometres away, which was too far for them to travel.

Hom learnt to count Buddhist beads as he recited prayers, and he did this regularly every day. He thinks it was the piety he showed that hastened his release, after five years rather than six. Time seemed to stand still for Hom in prison. He could take a walk on the veranda within the confines of the barbed wire. He could plant fruit trees such as bananas and papayas. He tried to complete a Shan-English dictionary, but it was confiscated when he was released. The magazines provided to Hom and other inmates had to be passed down the row of beds when they had finished reading them. One time, Hom forgot to pass a magazine on to the next bed and the occupant caught him by the collar and asked him belligerently if they belonged to his grandfather, as he hadn't handed them over to him.

Another altercation occurred when Hom was sitting near the foot of the stairs as his bed neighbour swept the upper floor, sending dust down the stairs. A scuffle followed and some older inmates came rushing to separate them. There was bound to be conflict when twenty-two people with different personalities were placed all together in one building for five or six years. When the guards came to investigate the fight, everyone blamed the other man, and he was taken away and placed in solitary confinement. Another time, when Hom had a fall and broke his arm, he was spoon-fed by one of my uncles – my father's younger brother. Hom had fractured his hand once before when he was in school. A doctor had fixed it then but it remained bent, so in prison the army doctor broke it again and put it right, without anaesthesia.

During Hom's five years of imprisonment, I saw him only three times. The first was when he was given permission to pay respects to his father at the Martyrs' Mausoleum on Martyrs' Day, held in remembrance of the day General Aung San and Hom's father were assassinated, along with seven others. We were allowed to take Hom home with us after the ceremony and I served him and the military intelligence officers some food. They refused it, and then they took him back to gaol.

Hom and his brother Kai laying a wreath at their father's tomb on Martyr's Day

The following day there was a picture on the front page the leading English-language newspaper, *The Nation*. The caption read: 'The detained martyr's son paying respects to his father'. The next day the newspaper's printing press was confiscated and its owner was prohibited from writing any anti-government articles.

The second time I saw Hom was when I was allowed to see him at the prison. A friend drove me there as I didn't want to involve my brothers or my brother-in-law. There was a certain fear in the community that any man could be arrested at any time for the least infringement. The hardest thing about seeing Hom again was that I had just had an attack of facial paralysis. I couldn't drink without spilling any liquid in a cup or glass; I couldn't exert myself; I couldn't smile or laugh. I could cry though. All I could do was cry when I saw Hom. We were given half an hour together. Then I was driven home.

It took me four or five months to be cured of this paralysis. I had to go to the base military hospital for treatment with a woman physiotherapist who was a major there.

The third time I saw Hom was again in the prison in the fifth year of his detention. My second-youngest brother, Sydney, drove me there. It was as emotional a meeting as the first. Again I was allowed to talk to Hom for half an hour. Then I came home, feeling desolate. However, about two months later, in 1967, about a week after we had celebrated our daughters' fifth and seventh birthdays, Hom was dropped home in a Datsun pick-up.

We were all about to have lunch at a family get-together. The rice was too soft and we had been thinking about Hom, as he likes soft rice. A new pot of rice was being cooked while the family waited at the table. Someone said, '*Pi* Hom would have loved that rice if he were here'. Then Hom's youngest brother, Kenneth, heard voices and went to the door to see who was in the pick-up, saying they must have been Mong Pawn Shans.

'One is definitely a Mong Pawn Shan,' he said. We all ran to the front door, except our second daughter Orawan. She held back, wondering what was going on because she couldn't remember her father. But happily, on that homecoming day, Hom was able to share in our family get-together.

We rang everyone to relay the message that Hom was home. We phoned my parents in Mandalay and the first thing my father said was not to give up my job. He knew that we were still living in precarious times. And it was true. Hom was not offered any job for two years as most people were afraid of employing a Shan chief who had just been released from custody.

Some freed political prisoners had no homes to go to. One had no wife to welcome him home as she and their children had gone underground during the six years he had been imprisoned. Another had lost his wife who had passed away from a heart attack, leaving eight daughters. It was sad.

Hom and some others had been released after five years upon signing a statement that said they would not take up politics again, not write anything against the government and not return to their homes in their various states.

Hom's freedom had come a year earlier than his uncle Hkio and my uncle Sao Sai Mong. But my uncle Sao Yawt Mong and some other detainees were imprisoned for seven years.

Chapter 8

Beauty, costume and grooming

My paternal grandfather and my father

Shan men look so handsome in their national dress.

Their traditional costume consists of a collarless shirt, long sleeves and cufflinks. The trousers are loose and worn with the top of the trousers held by being spread to each side above the hip and then folded in front, with the ends overlapping each other, and finally secured in place by a belt. The belts may be made out of leather cowhide or buffalo skin, or even silver or gold. The material the trousers are made of is usually hand-woven cotton, which is dyed beige by being dipped in boiling jackfruit bark.

On top of the shirt is worn a jacket made from the trouser material. It is open in the front with handmade buttons stitched on and loops made from the same material also sewn on. There are two side pockets and one smaller pocket on the left-hand breast to hold a gold or silver fob watch. We call the outfit a

Shan suit. The materials used to make these suits depend on the weather and how much a person can afford. The materials may be raw silk, black or white; they may be grey or beige woollen materials. The shoes are made from buffalo skin, the style being pump shoes. A Shan chief may even have worn silk pump shoes embroidered with gold thread.

There are accessories like the silk turbans, which are usually light pink, light yellow or cream, twelve feet long. The village men usually wear towels as turbans to keep their heads warm. Another accessory is a Shan bag slung over the shoulder. It is also hand-woven in black and red cotton or simply made from the beige cotton cloth.

For men's formal wear, a chief would wear a silk Shan suit and a long taffeta or brocade coat-like attire with gold or precious stone buttons. The ladies would wear silk *longyis* and silk jackets with the upper flap overlapping the lower one with loops for five buttons. The buttons were made of all kinds of precious stones including diamonds, which were set in gold with a small ring attached to it so that the loop could be secured to the fabric. They wore a stole on top. Nowadays girls do not wear them. They have modernised patterns and press studs or buttons are used.

For Shan women everyday wear is a bodice, on top of which a jacket made from hand-woven cotton is buttoned up in front with hand-woven buttons and loops. They can also wear jackets with a high neck, long sleeves and front flaps overlapping and buttoned up under the right arm. The sarong or *longyi* is made up of about one and a half metres of hand-woven material sewn together at the ends. A black cloth about four inches wide and one and a half metres long is stitched on the lap end. It is worn by holding it to one side of the hip, then folding the loose end over and tucking the corner tip into the hip. It stays in place through practised wear, or else a belt is used. Some of us use gold or silver belts. As for footwear, leather or velvet slippers are used daily and rubber flip-flops or wooden clogs serve as garden wear.

When we go out, especially on a visit to the monastery, we wear long-sleeved tops with a stole wrapped around our shoulders. The same outfit most often applies for formal wear.

Khemawadee in traditional dress

My grandfather Sao Intaleng's sister

My paternal grandmother and my Aunty Daphne
in ceremonial silk with gold and silver thread

The Burmese and people of the ethnic groups love flowers, so much so that women wear them in their hair most of the time. When you're around your garden and you fancy some bloom, you just pick it and put it in your hair. You can't resist. *Thazin* is a green-yellow orchid, tiny and dainty, which you wear in your hair, held by a small hairpin; *tharaphi* is a white fragrant flower from a low, broad-spreading tree, the *calophyllum amoenum*, which is worn as a garland in the hair.

We thread jasmine into a garland and wrap it around the knot of hair on the top of our head, and also into long garlands for the bride and groom at weddings, just as is done in India. Jasmine is also used as a flower for offerings, along with eugenia leaves and *zakawa*, a small yellow or white flower, and *zakazein*, a pastel green flower, both of which belong to the magnolia family.

Shan women are known throughout the region for their beautiful complexions. Burmese use *thanaka* ground into a fragrant cosmetic paste made from the bark and roots of *limonia acidissima.* A round and flat stone slab with a drain hewn out is used so that liquid can flow down a slightly sloping centre surface at the front. The bark of the *thanaka* is moved around and around with pressure, throwing in half a teaspoonful of water every now and then. The cream-coloured paste flows down the drain. You can grind until you get the amount you want. With your forefinger you scrape some off the surface and apply it on the forehead, another on each cheek, then on your nose and chin, and smooth it all over the face. Apply some to the ears and the neck. After rubbing with your finger evenly over the skin, the liquid is swabbed off with a piece of old cotton vest which is then washed properly. You need to just cover your face and pat it gently, not rub it. Then with the help of a small toothbrush you brush away the dried-up paste from your eyebrow. The affluent ladies would use an eyebrow pencil to accentuate the eyebrow line. Those in the village would use a burnt matchstick by making it wet with a touch of saliva. I remember watching my nanny doing that.

The paste can be made into a powder form and later applied with a square piece of cotton cloth. My grandmother and my younger aunts would always use *thanaka.* But my mother and her older sister didn't use it. Mum used a powder puff to apply talcum powder kept in a silver bowl on her dressing table, followed by a Yardley foundation cream and face powder. They both also used lipstick and perfume. When I reached the age of about seventeen my mother told me my face was too shiny, so as Yardley was not available by then, I would use Ponds vanishing cream until it too 'vanished', no longer imported after 1962 when the government nationalised many industries. So I reverted to *thanaka*, and still use it applied over a foundation cream.

Yardley lavender perfume was also my grandmother's favourite brand. However, she had a mixed paste of sandalwood, red sandalwood and some other fragrant woods made by a maid, and she would apply it all over the body to keep herself sweet-smelling. She would then adorn herself with a bodice which had pleated cups, then a cotton petticoat and a shimmy on top of which was a jacket made of organza or silk with precious stone buttons to match the sarong or *longyi*, under which a white underskirt or a cotton *longyi* was worn.

To complete it all, the hair in my grandmother's days was long and lustrous. The five virtues that a beautiful woman can be endowed with are perfect skin (the Burmese have a smooth brown skin while the Shan ladies have fairer complexions), perfect height that is neither too tall nor too short, lustrous jet black hair, eyes so lovely they might be compared to those of a doe, and beautiful pearly teeth. The hair is made clean and lustrous with the use of the crushed bark of a tree which resembles the hibiscus or hemp, soaked in water so that it becomes slimy. This thick liquid is mixed with boiled or roasted soap acacia bean, from a plant similar to a mimosa tree, and some lemon. The mixture is used for cleansing the hair of dirt and driving out evil spirits, and is also used for ceremonial purposes.

In the days of our kings and queens, Burmese women wore their hair on the crowns of their heads, wound into various knots underneath a smooth combed surface. The hair would often be piled very high, giving a woman a regal bearing. The ivory, tortoiseshell or gold combs needed to be about four inches long and half-moon shaped, often with at least three combs used.

Of course, the most important day in a woman's life for dressing should be her wedding day, when costume and grooming are undertaken with the assistance of one's closest family members to bring about the desired effect. My Aunty Pansy gave me her full attention on my wedding day.

Chapter 9

Recalling school days

Travelling home for school holidays

By the time I was ten my father had been appointed an administrator of the Hsipaw state and had taken up residence in a mansion allotted to the chief of that principality. The place was enormous, even for a family of eight and occasional house guests. It was a beautiful, ivy and honeysuckle-clad, double-storey building. My brothers and I enjoyed roaming all over the place, especially in the afternoons during which we were not allowed near the house as my father was taking a nap which he used to call 'forty winks'.

We would go punting on the pond, tease the monkey caged in the monkey house, have tea in the summer house or go to the river's edge to play with pebbles and swim in the shallow water. My father's assistant would send his three children, who were our age, to play with us. But we were to find that this idyllic period would soon be over.

When the members of the northern Shan state no longer wanted my father as their chief and he took up the post of chief mechanical engineer for the entire Shan states, the family moved to Lashio, the capital of the northern Shan states, about seventy kilometres from my birthplace, Hsipaw.

So for the next holiday we went to a new home and a new place to make new friends. There were three girls about my age who were all daughters of officers employed by the government.

Two of them were girlish and we played house together. One little girl was tomboyish and dressed in boys' clothing – a shirt and matching Shan pants. She preferred riding a bicycle and running over our earthen pots and pans to sitting and playing with them. But she became my best friend and still is to this very day. She is now a retired agricultural officer.

During one school term in 1949, when I was twelve, a crossfire battle took place between the central Burmese government troops and Karen rebel soldiers right around our school. There were bullets flying across the school grounds and I, along with all the boarders, had to move to the ground floor to a room at the centre of the campus so that no stray bullets would hit us. We had mattresses spread on the floor and spent days and nights confined to the gym, passing time by playing indoor games.

I don't recollect what the plight of my brothers was – where they stayed, for instance, whether they were in direct danger or how they survived. But I do remember my father's boss coming to pick up my brothers and me and taking us to live with his family, as no one was supposed to go into or out of the town.

A station wagon rolled through the cast iron gates of the convent honking 'oorooroot, oorooroot' and I recognised it as the sound of my father's car horn. My older cousins were jumping up and down, thinking my father had come to fetch them and me home. They cried with disappointment when they saw who stepped out of the car. It was my father's boss, the chief superintendent engineer for northern Burma, whom we knew as Uncle Tha Doke. In Burma we call our parents' friends 'uncle' and 'aunty' if they are in a certain age group. He had come to take my three brothers and me safely away from St Albert's high school to stay in his home for four whole months. He and his wife, Aunty Than, had three children about our age and they were expecting another one. Every morning after breakfast he would ring a bell to conduct a class. We had to do school lessons and it was a serious business because we were tested on what we had learnt.

On Sabbath days, that is the full moon days of each month, we did not have any classes but had to keep the eight precepts – including fasting after lunch until the next morning. Aunty Than served us cold drinks in the afternoons in case we were hungry. After the danger was over, we travelled back to our respective schools to join other students from the Shan states. A subdivision officer from Mong Yai had a permit to collect his sons from St Albert's, together with me, my cousins and their nieces who were the daughters of the chief of the principality of

South Hsenwi. The chief's wife, his Mahadevi, was a cousin of mine.

We all travelled in a truck, stopping to spend the night at Kyaukme, a town between Hsipaw, my birthplace, and Maymyo. The next morning we proceeded to Mong Yai where my parents came to meet us to take us on to Lashio where my father's head office was located. Oh, what a relief for our parents to see us safe and sound! My parents decided not to send us back to Maymyo because living there we were cut off from the main state. Instead my eldest brother was sent to Darjeeling and the three younger brothers and I were sent to another missionary school at Namtu, about seventy kilometres from Lashio.

The school, Our Lady's Convent, was administered by Italian nuns, but the teachers were Anglo-Indian, Karen and Italian nuns. The subjects – English, geography, history – were all taught in English. Burmese lessons were given by a half-Shan/half-Burmese who was not a graduate yet a brilliant teacher, even teaching us Shan as a subject. Catechism was also a compulsory subject.

The schoolhouse was a small double-storey building on a hilltop with a river dividing it from the main town. Namtu was a silver mining town and there were barren hillocks on one side of the river as a result. The great mounds of earth seemed lifeless except for the protruding chimneys of the smelters, from which smoke emerged. Bungalows were built on the hillsides. On the other side of the river was the commercial part of the town. Our school was on the same hillside where the bungalows were situated, overlooking the public works department's inspector's bungalow, the hospital, the church and the only bridge. So every morning and afternoon we schoolchildren would walk over the bridge. I had plenty of friends among my classmates and dormitory mates. The nuns were very strict: we were not allowed to speak in Burmese; we were confined to a certain area; we had to go to bed at a fixed time and get up together. As soon as we woke up, we washed ourselves, put on our uniforms, had breakfast and went off to class.

Breakfast was not appetising. Porridge cooked with jaggery (palm sugar) served on an enamel plate, it resembled something unmentionable. We never looked forward to lunch but we had to eat it. Onions boiled in vinegar is a dish that puts me off to this day. I can stand neither the smell of vinegar nor the taste of boiled onions. It was a great feast for us when we were served chicken curry, bean curd crackers or sometimes rice fried with peanuts.

After classes we had to change out of uniforms to play. The boys played football in the field on the lower level of the school grounds while girls would play a game or two of rounders. Then we had to freshen up and have dinner. We were allowed to have a bath only twice a week. After dinner we played games such as standing in a circle and singing 'a tisket a tasket' or 'ring a ring o' roses' or 'is the lamb at home?' I was about the oldest girl, with the others as young as four. After our games we'd say our prayers and off to bed.

On Thursdays we had to put our bedding in the sun, clean our beds, looking for bugs, and sweep the floor with brooms made from dry palm stems. Then we'd clean the floor with wet gunny bags. On Saturdays the nun in charge would let us go for a walk either up or down the hill, along a railway track built for trains to carry the silver ore. The refined form of this ore was made into blocks and shipped down to the capital, Rangoon, every week in the company's 'Dakota' aircraft, named 'The City of Bawdwin'.

Soon my days with the Italian nuns were numbered because the school only offered classes up to the 7th standard, equivalent to Year 10. Our parents arranged for us to go to the high school, Kambawsa College, in the southern Shan states, run by the board of Shan chiefs. The principal education officer of the Shan states was my uncle, Sai Mong, and his wife, my Aunt Mimi, was appointed as the principal of the school. It was established with the aim of administering discipline and guiding students within the Buddhist teachings. Since I had been in boarding schools all these years, my aunt thought it would do me good to live with her and her family and attend school from there. My parents decided that it was for the best, and I thought it was better than living with strangers or living like a nun. Even so, at the age of seventeen I would still cry when I was left with my uncle and aunt because I knew I would miss my mother.

As my parents had to see to the education of six children and my father was a government employee dependent on his salary alone, it was a relief for them that my uncle and aunt had taken on the responsibility of keeping me with them, together with another niece who was nine years old. They had two little daughters of their own aged five and three. Also living with us were two distant cousins of my aunt, the older of whom cooked and kept house for her while the younger was being trained to look after the baby who was expected to arrive during my stay there. I became friends with the younger cousin. The baby was a boy.

In the mornings the school car would pick us up and my aunt, her older daughter, her niece and I would travel to school about five kilometres to the southern end of the town. The school was located on level ground surrounded by hills. Cherry trees lined the roads leading to the school. The first sight that greeted you as you entered the grounds was a square building with a tiered roof shooting up towards the sky. This was the prayer hall where we would gather on Sabbath days to say our prayers, feed the monks and feast on the food that we'd all taken part in cooking the evening before. Then we would all go to the nearest monastery to say our prayers again and share our merits. That was just one of the school activities.

We would start our day in the assembly hall and stand in line according to the house we were allotted to. There were three houses: Ava, Tagaung and Kong-baung, being the names of ancient Burmese kingdoms. First we had to stand to attention, salute and then bend down out of respect for the Union of Burma and its flag. Second, we sang the Burmese national anthem followed by the Shan national anthem. Then we stood at ease to listen to an extract from famous writings read by the headmaster who was an Englishman. Extracts of news about world affairs were also included in the reading. After that, we proceeded to our various classrooms where six subjects, English, Burmese, geography, history, maths and general science, were taught by six different teachers. With the exception of Burmese, every subject was taught in English. My aunt taught geography and history.

We students had a very happy time making lots of new friends. We took part in house competitions, school athletics, basketball games and essay competitions within our school and in inter-school competitions. It was great fun going on picnics to the hot springs, to the lakes, and to the orange groves owned by my uncle-in-law who was chief of the principality of Lawk Sawk and whose youngest son was our classmate. Another time we travelled in cars and took a trip on Inlay Lake by motor boat. I remember the lake dwellers used their legs to row while standing at the stern of the boat. We visited various villages noted for their silversmith work, their hand-woven silk materials and their Shan bags. Houses were built on stilts and vegetable gardens were made on floating islands, which were formed by the accumulation of dried reeds piled high on matted bamboo. There was a marketplace where the sellers came to sell their wares in boats. In one village, a monastery housed five statues of Buddha famous for their powers. Every year there was a festival in mid-October when the statues were brought over to the town on the edge of a lake in a ceremonial royal barge, with the trustees, monks and lay people following in their own boats to the town. Hundreds of pilgrims would converge on the place. It was a beautiful and fantastic sight to witness. This land used to belong to the chief of Yawng Hwe, our first president of the

Union of Burma, Sao Shwe Thaike. Nowadays it is a major tourist attraction.

In Taunggy, we also took part in another celebration held every year, a light festival celebrated on the Sabbath towards the end of November. Burmese believe this is the month the full moon is at its largest for the year. People lit lanterns and oil lamps made from earthenware saucers which held oil with wicks of thick cotton thread. There was a competition of hot air balloons made to float into the night skies; the prettiest and the longest-lasting would win money in the competition. The balloons lit by oil or kerosene lamps were not elaborate and sturdy like modern hot-air balloons, but made of bamboo casing and Shan paper or parchment. The sheets of paper were made from some sort of reed or pulp from mulberry bark, and the glue was made of cooked rice powder.

Every day our lunches were brought over to our school at lunchtime in a metal tiffin carrier by the school bus driver. In the evening I would stay behind after school to take part in sports. On Buddhist Sabbath days we would all gather at the school's prayer hall, bedecked in our traditional finery, and then go to the monastery nearest to our school. It was altogether a completely different life than the one I had experienced with the nuns.

My uncle and aunt had a study with books piled ceiling-high. Now I regret not making use of the opportunity for reading. As a consequence of having to stay with strangers in my early days, I was afraid to enter strange rooms. My uncle and aunt were so well versed in the English language that I was almost too afraid to open my mouth in front of them in case I'd make a mistake. I used to tremble and be flustered just standing up in front of the class to read aloud. At the first school I attended we used to recite Burmese Buddhist prayers to begin the day. In the second and third schools, we sang 'God save the king' and said 'Hail Marys'. Thanks to my parents, after that we were old enough to leave school and go to university before the Burmese army seized power in a coup. Otherwise we would have had to pledge ourselves to the Burmese socialist government every morning to start our day.

When I was about seventeen, living at my Uncle Sai Mong and Aunt Mimi's home, I considered it not proper to go into their bedroom. One day Aunty Mimi's cousin, Aunty Su, who cooked and kept house, had a nail clipper and, spreading an old newspaper on the floor, started cutting her nails. The Burmese use newspaper so that their nail cuttings won't touch the earth. They're superstitious about that happening. When Aunty Su had finished, I took the clipper from her and began to cut my nails too. No sooner had I begun than my uncle came up the stairs and went straight to his bedroom in search of the clippers. I pushed the pair of clippers into Aunty Su's hand and told her to hand them over to him. She refused to do so. The clippers were in my hands when he came into our room and he promptly scolded me for not putting them back in their place. That was the first time I'd gotten myself into trouble since the incident over the pencil stub. Oh what a wicked girl I was! I certainly felt my misdemeanours deeply.

Chapter 10

Siblings aplenty

Considering we were six siblings and there were more than sixty first cousins in our family, the naming of children was a serious task. All over the world names are important to parents and children alike. Since a name is attached to a person for life, it's necessary for parents to select names with love and care.

In Burma, name-giving ceremonies are usually held one month after a baby is born. As well as immediate family members attending, guests include close friends of all ages, who are invited to partake of some breakfast of fish soup and rice noodles. Or perhaps the guests may like chicken soup with coconut milk accompanied by wheat noodles.

There will be some Buddhist monks present to chant prayers, bestowing their blessings on the household members and the guests gathered to celebrate the naming of the child. The monks will be fed first with rice and curry, which is sustaining as a meal. Then many sweet dishes will be offered to them before the lay people are served.

The name of the newborn will be discussed over the meal. As soon as the guests hear a name they will know what day the baby was born and whether it is a girl or a boy. In the days of our kings, names would indicate in which family the baby belonged.

As I've already related, we are a superstitious people who believe in astrologers, fortune-tellers, psychics, prophets, spirits and celestial beings. Not only do we choose our names according to the day on which a baby is born, we also study the stars under which a baby is brought into the world. Pretty names such as the names of flowers and sensitive emotions, for example 'tender' and 'graceful', are reserved for girls. Boys are given masculine names such as 'strength', 'warrior' and 'courage'.

In earlier times, we did not have official government birth certificates. Instead, the day and the date of birth, together with the astrological signs, were inscribed on a palm leaf using a stylus, written by either a renowned monk or a recognised astrologer. However, for the naming ceremony of two of my brothers and for me, the names were chosen by my great grandfather's sister, known to us as 'great grandmother', because she was the oldest in the family and would ask celestial beings to show her the names to be given to newborns.

In our case, I was not named until I was aged about two, Tony when he was three and Bunny at age one. I've been told that as part of the ceremony we three were seated on a mattress-like cushion and adorned with traditional clothes and gold headbands on which our names were inscribed. We were blessed by a monk, a Brahmin priest and the older members of the clan. They showered presents on us, especially jewellery. My father did not have a job at that time and we were not as well-to-do as some others, so the presents were not as elaborate or expensive as in earlier times. For example, when my mother was named, she would have received jewellery, orange groves and paddy fields.

My name is a Pali word, Sao Khemawadee, meaning a sanctuary with no worries. After World War II we were sent to missionary schools, and since the nuns and the priest preferred English names, I was then known as 'Biddy', the name given to me by an Australian friend of my parents whose husband worked in forestry. I'd always been addressed by relatives and friends as Biddy since I'd been a babe in arms.

Most of the children in our family were given European names simply because European teachers at the schools they attended couldn't pronounce their Shan names. So whatever name might appeal to a teacher at any given time would be conferred on the child and it would stick for life.

When we had to fill in forms to sit for our matriculation examination, we were required to give our official names. We do not have surnames and keep our personal names when we are married. My husband and I are addressed by our individual names, not a family name in common. When my husband went to Fiji to work as a UN employee, he was called 'Mr Hom', as staff thought his personal name, which is always written last, was his family name. Here in Australia during immigration interviews, we had to state our family names, whereby my husband became 'Mr Sao', whereas 'Sao' is actually a title used by those who belong to the family of the ruling chiefs. I was called Mrs Hom. But when we rented a home, the landlord called me 'Mrs Soya', a mix-up of the name 'Sao', so I would joke about having become a soya bean!

As I said, in my family there were six children – five boys and myself, a girl wedged in between the first and third sons. We four older children went to the same school until after World War II, when the boys then had to lodge with my father's old teacher, Mr Nicholas, in Maymyo, and I was sent to live with my father's friend U Lu Din's family, also in Maymyo.

We would look forward to holidays when we would all be together again. I remember the holidays in my later childhood most clearly. It would either be the winter or summer holidays because the October holidays were too brief a period for us to go home. My father would either come for us or send someone to take us home.

It was always in the late afternoons that we were homeward bound. The fields would be bare after harvesting of the crops. Or the land might be cleared and the grass cut, with the cut branches of the trees burnt to prepare for the cultivation of the next crop – otherwise known as 'slash and burn' cultivation, which was common on the Shan plateau at the time. I distinctly remember the smell of burning leaves and the fresh air tinged with smoke as we travelled home at dusk.

When we arrived home we would have a thorough scrub and wash to get ready for my mother's cooking. We would have dinner together and then sit around the fireplace where a wood fire had been kept burning since early evening. We'd have roasted chestnuts or sunflower seeds and oranges, the shells and peels of which were thrown into the fire. The orange skins kept the mosquitoes away. We would chat until late even after my father had gone to bed.

My mother saw to it that we were all fed four meals a day, with lunch and dinner the substantial meals. For us, breakfast consisted of rice porridge or glutinous rice, whereas Dad preferred bacon and eggs. He liked to buy a leg of pork and cut, cure and smoke it into bacon and ham himself, yet we had a cook and his assistants with us, even when we had the Japanese at our heels. The cook's assistants would walk to a village a mile or two away and return carrying a basket full of glutinous white and purple rice and round sesame seeds. The rice would be steamed, and when it was cooked it would be placed in a mortar and pounded with a pestle with roasted ground sesame and salt thrown in at intervals. Then it would be flattened out on a round tray lined with banana leaves. It could be eaten either while fresh and hot, or once it had hardened be cut into three-inch cubes, threaded onto bamboo skewers and roasted on hot embers. We would sit around the fireplace and peel off the crispy crusts and eat them, then press the remaining cake and toast it again to again peel off the crust to eat it, over and over. It went on until the last bit was too small to be toasted. We had all the time in the world to linger over this luxury.

Once when we were in a country town called Hsum Hsai, my brothers and I would explore places around the village, crossing streams that flowed through the paddy fields or taking a dip in them, not bothered about the rain or sun, the mud or grime. There would be fish and leeches in the water. We would catch tiny crabs from the streams, or tadpoles from the puddles. In summer there were burnt fields from which wild asparagus plants with fresh young leaves would spring up, so we would pick them to take home for dinner.

At the end of summer the monsoon season would begin, lasting from May to October. With the first showers, mushrooms would shoot up. Our cook would call out to the household members and the neighbours, 'The sun is shining, so let's go and pick the mushrooms.' So we'd join him in a mushroom-picking tour around the village. The group would come home laden with baskets full of mushrooms. My mother used to make mushroom stir fries or pickle them, packed in banana leaves with hot cooked rice and left overnight, to be served with crisp-fried onions and garlic for lunch the next day. We also picked wild flowers, especially eugenia leaves for the altar.

Market day fell only once in five days so we depended for food mostly on whatever was grown in the fields or the garden. In the paddy fields, we children used to jump down from the short rice silos and tall rice foliage haystacks which were kept for feeding the cows, precious as they supplied us with fresh milk. We used nylon parachutes left over from the food drops of World War II in our games, holding onto them as we'd jump down from the haystacks, pretending we were jumping out of planes, just as we'd seen the Allied food bundles float down to us. And we'd play in the barns where rice, peanuts, potatoes and coffee seeds were stored.

At the beginning of every monsoon season a rice-growing ceremony was held. My parents would initiate the ritual activity to the beat of the Shan drums, cymbals and gongs.

For meat and protein, my father would go hunting and fishing with the village menfolk, and my eldest brother used to tag along. They'd shoot wild pigs, deer and game birds. Our fish was always freshwater fish, caught by divers after a dynamite stick was thrown into the dykes.

As for the water supply, there were no reservoirs or pipelines. A water carrier with drums mounted on carts pulled by bullocks would travel from our village to a pond fed by spring water which flowed into a stream. The men would make several trips to fetch the water and fill tubs for cooking, drinking and cleaning. Our maids went to the stream to wash clothes and bathe. Sometimes we would also go to bathe at a stream. There were a lot of bathing spots in the vicinity of the village, but the ponds were reserved for drinking. A bamboo pole or two would be installed in such a way that water flowed from the ponds through the bamboo onto the spots where we could bathe and wash clothes, using stone slabs or wooden planks for standing or sitting as we chatted.

For modesty, women wore their *longyis* wrapped up around their chests while they bathed, and men would also bathe wearing *longyis*. Even we children wore clothing as we danced about in the water – *longyis* for girls and shorts for boys.

Chapter 11

Tony – a reserved fellow

Of my five brothers, shall I begin with the story of the eldest? His name was Sao Kan Gyi, though he was always known as Tony among relatives and friends. He was born on 8 April 1935, a Monday. As I've mentioned, he was considered so precious that when he was born no one was allowed to toot the car horn in case the sound gave him a shock.

Tony was born in the white *haw* or mansion, and being the firstborn, everybody, including our grandmother and younger aunts, doted on him. My aunt Sao Thu Nandar gave him a solid gold plate when he was one month old, perhaps because she didn't have any children herself and wanted to celebrate this special birth of her firstborn nephew. Later she became his godmother.

He was a year and a half older than me. When he was about eight, we moved to Nawng Khio, where we lived in a house on stilts. The upper level was a living area and the lower level was a place for us to play. Mostly we'd play sedately, but one afternoon Tony overreacted and caused a stir.

He was under the house splitting a stick of bamboo with a knife when the son of the township officer came towards him on his bicycle and cycled over Tony's hat, which was lying near him. Instantly, Tony struck the boy with his knife. The boy dropped his bicycle, and holding his bleeding head, ran across the marketplace to his home. The whole market was in a commotion, people passing on word from one seller to another, that the administrator's son had hacked the township officer's son.

Dad heard the uproar, strode home and whipped Tony until he wet his pants. Then he made him stand behind the sofa in one corner of the sitting room without food for an hour or so. When it was time for everybody to have dinner, our cook took some food and fed him without Dad's knowledge.

When he was aged about nine, Tony was sent to the Buddhist monastery to learn some prayers and to read and write in Burmese. There was no actual school there, and most of the day he spent playing with the little monks or novices. Once he was so engrossed in playing that he didn't want to go home even though he wanted to go to the toilet. He stood there crossing his legs – but not for long. He dirtied his pants and the little monk had to take him home. That's how stubborn he was.

Another instance of trouble that I clearly remember occurred in Hsum Hsai, where my father was posted as administrator. My younger brother, Bunny, made a square spinning top from a potato with a piece of bamboo running through it. He then drew the figures of an eel, a pig, a chicken and a frog. Tony, the nannies and I sat around while Bun spun the top and covered it with a bowl so we couldn't see which picture was on the top. Using Japanese currency notes left over from the war, we would bet on which animal would be seen after the top was spun. When Bun lifted up the bowl, if the pig was on show, for instance, he would have to double the money for whoever had bet on the pig.

Right then, the top fell through a crack in the timber floor. Only Bunny could go under the house in search of the top because the floor wasn't high enough for the older children to fit. One of the nannies held the kerosene lamp, tilting it so that Bun could see. But she tilted it too much and the floor caught fire, ignited by the kerosene.

Everyone was shouting 'fire, fire!' Dad came rushing in, very angry that his meeting with the township officers should be disrupted by the noise at the other end of the house. He simply grabbed Tony, lifting him up off his feet and gave him a thrashing in front of the officers. As a result, Tony became even more stubborn. Bun got away because he was hidden under the house.

Soon after, Tony was sent to an all boys' school, St Albert's school in Maymyo, together with Bunny and Tim, my younger brothers, and Louis, my cousin whose father was my father's older brother who had passed away.

As the boarding department at the school was not ready after the disruption caused by World War II, the boys at first had to live with Dad's old teacher, Mr Nicholas. They lived there for a year and they were not happy. When the boarding department was ready, they were pleased to be placed there.

My school, St Joseph's convent, was further out of town than St Albert's. After the crossfire of bullets at my school in fighting between Karen rebels and government forces in 1949 and our escape back to our parents in Lashio, they decided not to send us back to Maymyo. My younger brothers and I were sent to a smaller and poorer school in Namtu while Tony was sent to St Joseph's College in Darjeeling, which was run by the Jesuit Brothers. He was there for three years. Then the government changed its policy of sending money abroad, so Tony was brought home along with other Burmese boys.

It was in 1952 that the Shan chief's school was reopened in Taunggyi, not only for the chief's sons and nephews as in the past but also for the sons and daughters of the townsfolk. Tony and Bunny were enrolled there. Tony had some trouble relearning Burmese, the only compulsory subject. All other subjects were taught in English.

The following year Tony and Bunny were joined by Tim and me. They were boarders at Kambawza College while I stayed with my uncle and my aunt-in-law, who was the principal of the school. Tony, Bunny and I were all in the same class, studying for the matriculation exam. All three of us passed, Bunny in the first division, Tony in the third division, and I in the second division grades. Education was valued highly in our family, so Dad and Mum were proud parents as they drove us the four hundred miles down to attend university in Rangoon.

At university, Tony took up arts subjects and passed every year, gaining his Bachelor of Arts in four years. He began to work as an English tutor while attending Bachelor of Law classes.

By this time, Mum and Dad had moved to Rangoon to live in a huge house, so Tony moved back home, sharing a room with Gerry, our youngest brother. Tony and three other male tutors were recruited by the information department, where he was given the job of editor of the government-owned *Forward* magazine.

Tony loved music and books. He was also a stickler for routine. As soon as he got up in the morning he would turn on the radio to listen to music, then he would have breakfast, have a bath and go to work. In the evening after work he would take a bus and then walk home, have a bath and sit down and drink until 8 pm sharp when he would have dinner. He would listen to the news, then to light music and at 10 pm exactly he would switch off his radio and go to bed.

I remember once in the 1970s when Dad and Mum came to stay with us, Tony dropped in to visit. As usual, he went straight to the bar and poured himself a drink, little knowing that Dad had filled the decanter with Shan tea. Dad nudged Mum, and after Tony had taken a sip, Dad asked, 'How is it?'

'Not bad. A little light though,' Tony replied.

Dad and Mum held back their laughter. Dad often liked to play practical jokes on others. The incident has stayed in my mind, perhaps because it was indicative of Tony's cool nature.

For sport when he was young, Tony used to play tennis. Later it was more fashionable to play golf so he would tag along with Dad when he played golf in Lashio. Down in Rangoon, Tony had no exercise except for that little walk between the bus stop and his house.

His office was five storeys high and he had to climb the stairs every day as there was no elevator. An outcome of this exertion was that he had a heart attack at the age of 45 and had to take rest for a month. Before the heart attack, I'd been wondering why he used to take a rest at three different places as he'd walk up the hill about 500 metres to the bus stop near our home. This was when he'd moved in with us for a while in the mid-1970s after Mum and Dad moved to Mandalay. After that, he bought a small house in Eighth Mile, about a mile from our place.

When he had the heart attack, I blamed myself for having made him move out. He might not have passed away if he had stayed on with us and eaten the food I cooked instead of the food cooked by his housekeeper and her husband.

It was strange that he never married, and I think it was because Mum didn't like the girls he admired. She didn't even like my aunt making a match with some girls. He might have lived longer if he had acquired a wife to look after him. Mum had spoiled him so much he couldn't take care of himself.

The day of his death in February 1977, Tony had dropped in at our place as it was Hom's birthday, and he was very well dressed for the occasion. He explained that he'd had some new shirts made and was wearing one.

After drinks and dinner, Hom's best friend, John Khun Kyi, drove Tony home, dropping him at the path that Tony usually took before proceeding on to his own home. At two o'clock in the morning, my cousin Gladys, who lived next door to Tony, phoned me, saying she didn't know what was wrong with Tony but the boy who lived with him had alerted her that Tony was in a bad way, suffering some pain. Hom, Dad, Mum and I went to see for ourselves. When we got there, Mum and Dad went in to see him and called a doctor who lived at Tenth Mile, two miles away, and he came and pronounced Tony dead.

I had never seen anybody die. I couldn't help hugging tight the main solid teak pillar that supported the roof, trying to slow my heart beat.

As I said, he was only 45 years old and I could imagine how Mum and Dad felt to have one of their children die before them.

Tony's ex-classmates and work colleagues came to decorate his coffin. He was greatly loved, especially by the older ladies who were our Aunt Millie's classmates. But I feel it was a great pity Tony never shared a special love with any particular woman and took her as his wife.

Chapter 12

Bunny – a good-hearted gambler

Bunny with wife, Alvina, in the United States in the 1980s

Bunny was born on 24 March 1938 in Kengtung, my father's birthplace. He was named Sao Kan Kywe but as an adult changed his name to Sao Kawn Kiao Mangrai, my grandfather's name, to show that he was a Shan not a Burmese. Yet even after the name change he was always known as 'Bunny' or 'Bun', the nickname given to him from birth by my parents.

He was a Saturday-born and Saturday births are regarded as reserved for those endowed with special virtues. Therefore the stars of the parents may be either overshadowed by their child's birth or enhanced if the parents are also Saturday-borns. If the baby is a firstborn, the above belief applies. But if the parents are Sunday-borns, as Mum and Dad were, a Saturday child shouldn't affect them. Actually Saturday-borns are so fortunate that the rest of the family is cast in the shadows. Thank God our Bun wasn't a firstborn.

As I've said, Dad was appointed an administrator for the principality of Kengtung state after his eldest brother, the chief, had been assassinated by his nephew in 1937, and the state was in need of a ruler because the heir to the chieftainship was still very young. However, my father's sister-in-law – who was also my mother's first cousin – tearfully approached Colonel Robert – the resident assigned to oversee the welfare of the eastern Shan states by the British government – and told him to retract the appointment as her own son would be deprived of chieftainship should my father refuse to relinquish his post as administrator.

So my parents decided to leave Kengtung and go back to Mum's principality, Hsipaw, when Bun was just forty-five days old. In these early days, Mum mixed up Bunny's birthdate as being her own, but Dad looked up a 100 year old calendar and found that Mum's birthday was 14 March. She was vague about dates, being confused about another son's birthdate some years later, saying Gerry was born 'when they bombed the Goakhteik Bridge'.

Bunny was a sickly baby and was fed a fixed amount at fixed times according to the family doctor's instructions. He was therefore hungry all the time. He would pick up any kind of food and eat it, for which he would get a beating. During World War II when the Japanese occupied Burma, the maids at home would lay out the breakfast table the previous night so that we could grab breakfast as soon as we got up, before the bomber planes appeared in the sky. One morning the long loaf of bread was missing. A rat wouldn't have been able to carry it away, we knew. So the maids went to look for it under Bun's pillow, and sure enough, there it was. He had dug a hole into his pillow to hide it. So Bun was given a beating again. He became very stubborn after so much beating.

When my father was appointed the administrator of Hsipaw principality, he was welcomed by the people. They had built a podium from which Dad was to give an acceptance speech, and steps were built for him to walk up. Bun followed him with a cap worn with the peak to the back, not a good look in the 1940s. He was pulled down by the state police and held until the body guard told them he was the administrator's son.

In the Shan states it was customary to have fairs at the festival grounds. The festivals took place at least four times a year, the most prominent being the Baw Gyo Pagoda Festival. Stalls were allotted to those who wanted to sell their wares or to have gambling stalls. One of the stalls that attracted children had pictures of animals laid out on a thick square plastic sheet. This was the same game of 'spin the top' that we played at home, so it was very enticing to children.

A square top, usually made of ivory with pictures of animals on each side, was spun and covered with a bowl. A person could put his money on one animal and win three times the amount if the bowl was removed and displayed that animal's picture. In some gambling dens there might be as many as thirty-six animals to choose from, with a win being twenty-seven times the amount you might bet. Sometimes the thirty-six animal pictures might be spread all over the body of the image of a spirit. Then pictures of the thirty-six animals on thirty-six cards were placed in a canvas bag with a drawstring threaded through the top so that it could be pulled tightly and tied. Only one card would be placed in the bag and pulled up a pole while the remaining thirty-five animals stayed down. In the evening at 6 o'clock the bag was brought down and opened for the win.

Many people became addicted to this type of gambling, and often the addiction would begin during childhood. I was tight-fisted, preferring to walk around the fairgrounds, spending only a little money eating roasted sunflower seeds, a puffed rice cracker or peanuts roasted in their shells and sold in paper cones, rather than waste my money on betting.

Bun preferred the gambling. He made a top out of a diced potato, drew some animals on it and sat at a market stall on market day which fell every fifth day. He would spread out the sheet of paper and start spinning the top. Word soon circulated that the administrator's son had opened a four-animal spinning stall. When Dad heard about it, Bun got another beating.

Bun was the most intelligent person in our family. He caught up with Tony and me in his studies when we were in the same school in the same class in 1953. When we all sat the matriculation exam, only Bunny gained a first division place, standing second in the whole of the Shan states. Bun was awarded a scholarship by the Shan government, whereby he obtained a sum of money in addition to the pocket money that was provided to us. That year our parents were the proudest couple in the town of Lashio.

Bun went to medical school at the University of Rangoon for two years. But unfortunately he got into the habit of playing cards instead of studying and didn't take his exams. So he couldn't continue his studies and transferred to study English literature, political science and western history, graduating with a Bachelor of Arts degree. He worked as an English tutor and continued to study law.

Then he met and married a fellow tutor, Alvina Wales, and worked as a manager for a government-owned chain of stores.

When Bun became a member of the Burma Socialist Program party, he had to undergo training at the Burma Socialist Party camp and was then posted to Kengtung as the general manager of the People's Properties Company. He was very principled. For example, he made a rule that his wife was not to wear batik *longyis,* in case the townspeople assumed that he had been supplying her with clothes that customs had confiscated from black marketeers. He also refused to exchange the not-so-good-quality rice he'd bought from the people's shop for the much better rice that my aunt Sao Bo Sawan offered to give him.

In the end, he was disappointed when he was not elected as the township president of the Burma Socialist Party. He gave up his job and returned to Rangoon to apply for immigration to Australia, but the Burmese government's policy at that time meant he was not issued with a passport. The Australian embassy turned him down even though his wife had an English maiden name, 'Wales'. He was asked, 'Why don't you change your name to Mr Green?', which he considered a rude comment. He became so angry that he withdrew his application. Instead he applied for migration to the United States and managed to migrate there via Hong Kong.

In San Francisco he worked as a taxi driver for one day only, after he was held around the throat from the back seat by a passenger who demanded the day's takings at knife point. Bun gave up the money and took the taxi back to the depot, where he handed it over and told them he would not be driving again.

He then applied for a police officer's job as a crime scene investigator in Concord about seventy kilometres away. The police department was impressed with his resume and his fluency in spoken and written English. It helped that he knew a lot about human anatomy and had studied law.

Bunny worked in the police department for twenty-five years. One day he was driving at work when he felt ill and pulled over to the side of the road for a while. The next morning Bun found himself swollen all over and was diagnosed in hospital as having congestive heart failure. He lived on for several years. Then one day he cleaned out the pantry, took some tinned provisions to homeless people, went on to play golf, had a nap in the afternoon, and in the evening went to a meeting. He felt tired as he was giving a speech, so his son continued the speech. As Bun sat down, with his arm resting over his wife's shoulder, he passed away.

Who can say what will occur in anyone's life, the ups and downs that must be faced, whether a person is intelligent or dull-witted, wealthy or poor? At least I can say my brother Bun enjoyed his life, with five children and a loving wife. And he had the intuition, determination and gambling spirit to leave Burma in order to live a better life in the West even though he loved the Shan people.

Chapter 13

Tim – the loner

Tim in Edinburgh in his teens

When Tim was born on September 1939 in Hsipaw, my mother believed that he was the reincarnation of her brother-in-law Sao Ohu Kyar, the chief of Hsipaw, because he'd loved her so much he'd have wanted to reincarnate as her child, she thought.

The baby was named Sao Khun U, 'Khun' meaning 'ruler', but was always known as Tim.

He was sensitive, shy, clingy and scared of ghosts. He would hang on to Mum's *longyi* when she and Dad dropped us all off at boarding school. Tim would find any excuse to cry for two days before we left for school.

Whenever Tim received something new, even a pair of shoes, he would put them under his pillow. He was reluctant to part with any of his possessions.

After he attended St Albert's school, he transferred with me to Our Lady's Convent and Kambawza College in Taunggyi. From Kambawza College, Tim was selected along with another outstanding student, Lawrence Thar, to study in England on a scholarship offered by Burma Oil Company (BOC). In those days Burma was rich in oil and petroleum products.

However, Tim was studying in Edinburgh and about to enter university when the Burmese government took control of BOC and cut off his scholarship allowance. It was a cruel blow. Tim had to leave school and start working as an accountant at Michelin Tyres in London in 1952. His salary was too good for him to relinquish and go back to his studies. He would never again see our parents.

A Burmese gentleman had introduced Tim to a certain lady and her daughter, hoping he would marry the daughter. Instead he became attached to her mother. I think he might have wanted someone to lean on as a mother. He shared a flat with the woman, Maureen, in London, and they used to drive to Wales at weekends to stay at the cottage farm he had bought.

Every year on Burmese Independence Day, he would attend a reception held at the Burmese embassy in London. On one occasion he overheard the ambassador telling some Burmese guests to stay clear of him as he was an ex-Shan rebel, so he stopped going to the receptions. The ambassador, who had lived next door to us in Rangoon before he moved to London, must have mistaken Tim for my second-youngest brother, Sydney, who went underground in Burma. But Tim was worried and stopped renewing his Burmese passport.

But in 1970 when an aunt and uncle of mine went to London for eye treatment, they asked Tim, 'Why don't you visit your parents? They are getting on in age.' So Tim went to the Burmese embassy with my uncle, who introduced him to the new ambassador and the military attaché. Tim requested that his passport be renewed. He wrote to Mum and Dad to say that his passport would be ready in a few months, and he would be able to visit them in Burma. Mum was looking forward to his visit.

But Tim didn't make the trip. I don't know why not. Then when we were living in Fiji, I wrote to him that it would be easier to visit us and see Mum there. He didn't make a move or explain why he wouldn't come. When we came to Australia, again I wrote to Tim saying we were here to stay permanently, and asking him whether he would like to visit us.

He replied that he would take an early retirement and come over to Australia to stay with a close friend of his. He planned that we'd all then proceed to Burma. Mum flew out to Bangkok to meet him. But he never came.

Almost a decade later, the news of his death came as a shock to me. It was on 18 January 2001 that Tim was found dead in his flat, aged fifty-eight. The gas was still on; the smell was overwhelming. A doctor was called to check him, and pronounced that Tim had passed away three weeks earlier – which meant that he had died about 28 December, three days after Christmas. What made it even harder to accept was that we believe he'd died on the same date of the month that Bun had died two years earlier. It was the Christmas season, so why wasn't his partner with him at the time?

My brother Sydney flew to London to attend to Tim's burial. The funeral parlour said that as it was winter there were a lot of deaths, and it would be three weeks before Tim could be buried. As Sydney only had one week's leave, he couldn't stay on in London. Tim's partner met Sydney to show him Tim's will stating that everything he owned had been left to her, and she handed over an old leather briefcase filled with his photographs. A nephew of my mother who lived in London took charge of the funeral procedures and organised a small wake for friends.

Tim had been away from home for forty years and during that time there had been little contact with any of us. How could a person who was my mother's favourite son, and who wouldn't let go of her skirt when as a boy he was deposited at the boarding school, become the one who detached himself from our family? I could understand his attachment to an older woman when he was away from home and needed a mother figure. But years later, if she had the same attachment for him, why was he left to die alone – especially at Christmas? I couldn't ever understand that. Yet it was the life he chose, or was chosen for him.

Those of us who were still alive after his death felt desolate, and I wondered about the separate fates of all of our family members, fates which, after the military coup, had cast us out of our homeland and, as if in a terrific storm, had flung us across the oceans of the world.

Chapter 14

Sydney – an independence fighter

Sydney in the early 1970s

Sydney was born on 1 May 1941. You may have noticed that this means he was born on Labour Day and it's true that he has laboured all his life.

He also happened to be born at the bottom of the stairs because my mother couldn't make it up the stairs in time. At the foot of the stairs there was a day bed, so as he was impatient to be born, the whole stairwell had to be quickly converted into a labour room made from patchwork curtains and tapestry screens.

He was given the name Yan Paing, meaning 'to conquer enemies'. At home he was called Swy meaning 'serious-minded'. But when, at the age of seven, he joined us at Our Lady's Convent in Namtu, the nuns called him Sydney. I don't know why.

After we older siblings left for Rangoon to attend university, Sydney went on to Kambawza College. But Dad withdrew him from Kambawza when he was about to take the matriculation exam because he was given a caning by the headmaster as punishment for challenging the school captain. Dad used to cane his children but he objected to someone else caning them. So Sydney attended the Guardian Angels' Convent as a day student, walking about half a mile from home each day. The convent was run by nuns who belonged to the same order as those in Namtu, but it was bigger and had a high school. Sydney passed his matriculation exam at that school.

He was studying international relations honours at the University of Rangoon at the time the military took over government in Burma in 1962. He had a hostel room at Mandalay Hall which faced the student's union building on Chancellor Road. Early on 7 July 1962 the army bombed the union building and razed it to the ground. It was lucky that Sydney and my husband Hom's sister Myint were at our house at the time.

The next day I told them to go back to their respective hostels to get their bedding and clothing. Sydney was almost there when he heard the rattling of Bren light machine guns firing. He jumped into an open drain by the side of the road and lay flat on his belly. A fellow student in front of him was not quick enough to duck. He was killed. Sydney found his room at the hostel in a mess, he said. The ceiling had fallen on his bed. Fortunately, because he'd spent the night with us at home, he had cheated death again – as he'd also been saved years before during WW II when he'd been at our aunt's place as our compound in Hsum Hsai was bombed.

Another time he came close to death was when he was confined to bed with typhoid at the age of about twelve. At first he spent time recovering at the convent where I was also a student. We girls had to take turns scrubbing the floor, which allowed me to sneak him in some preserved ginger when I was down on my knees cleaning near his bed. After a few weeks, he had a relapse and had to be taken back to hospital in Namtu, where Bunny was also confined with typhoid. In those days, about 1952, anti-typhoid medicine was scarce so medication had to be transported from Rangoon. A friend of our parents, who was the agent for Union of Burma Airways and the Burma

Corporation, requested a pilot to send the medicine on the very next flight. It arrived in time to save their lives and a few weeks later they were both taken home to recuperate.

My father had been asked by the hospital doctor which son should be favoured with the medicine as there wasn't enough for two. My father's response was that they should be administered equal amounts as he loved them equally. As fate would have it, there was enough medication to cure them both.

Graduating from university in 1965 with an international relations honours degree, Sydney applied for a post at the foreign office since he thought it was appropriate for his qualifications. But when he went for an interview, he was told by one member of the public service commission, 'You Shans don't need jobs. Why don't you go underground?'

Sydney worked at the German embassy for a year or two and lived with us while my husband was in prison. In the mornings on the way to work, he would pick up a driver at my aunt and uncle's house, and hand the car over to him when he got off at the embassy so the driver could take me on to university and my two girls to their school, to be picked up again at the end of the day. Sydney would hand over his salary to me every month to help me out with the household expenses. After my husband was released from detention, Sydney stayed on with our family for a while. Then, tired of bowing and cowering to the German officers at the embassy, he went home to Lashio to look after our parents' house while they were living in Mandalay at the match factory.

He took charge of a little rice mill owned by my father which had been moved to Se En. While there, Sydney would hear horses' hooves and people passing by the mill during the night. They were independence rebels on the move and he made contact with them.

One day in 1968, Sydney visited my mother's best friend in Lashio with a young woman. They stayed there for one night and said they would take a bus to Hsipaw. But my Aunty Millie said Sydney did not visit her in Hsipaw. The bus driver said the two got off halfway between Lashio and Hsipaw, which meant that they'd alighted from the bus at the place where our father's rice mill was located. A friend who helped look after the mill said he did not recall seeing Sydney. Later we found out that Sydney had been requested to escort the girl from Kengtung to her boyfriend who'd gone underground in the jungle. At first it was a mystery to us, but later we came to understand that Sydney had chosen to join the Shan State Independent Army and fight for Shan independence.

Sydney was in the jungle for about nine years. He had met a young woman from Hsipaw who joined him in the jungle, and they married and had two children during this time. They lived under harsh conditions, coping with lice, leeches, snakes and heavy rain and avoiding tigers, wild boar and malaria. They mostly ate raw pumpkin, rice and native bamboo shoots, and during the cold season it was a bitter existence. His work involved serving boiled rice or rice porridge to his colleagues. After a time, there was a split among the co-rebels, with some going to the extreme of practising Marxism, others wanting to join Khun Hsar, the drug warlord, and still others staying in the original group.

Sydney and his friend Tzang, known as 'elephant' in Shan, remained with the original group to fight purely for Shan independence. In 1976 Tzang left the army to settle down in Chiang Mai in Thailand.[9] About a year later, Sydney also left the army to have a medical check-up in Chiang Mai. One evening he and his friend witnessed their superior officer being shot at after being invited to dinner by another disaffected rebel in the town. Neither wanted to end up with the same fate.

So Sydney changed his name to Singhadej, with a family name of Pengrai after the registration office got the spelling of Mangrai wrong, and stayed in Chiang Mai with his family. Later he moved to Bangkok where he worked for a ceramics factory making traditional blue and white-patterned ceramics, a job that our aunt-in-law found for him.

Later he worked for a German scaffolding and screw manufacturing business but was laid off with one and a half years' pay when he turned sixty.

Sydney was diagnosed with cancer so now he follows a strict macrobiotic diet and exercises, playing tennis, swimming and walking every day, which he believes has protected him from any recurrence of the illness.

He continues to work for recognition of the Shan people in their own right. He's travelled to Japan, and in 2012 he went to Washington to give a talk on discrimination against the Shan by the Burmese government, describing the parlous state of ethnic minorities living along the border with Thailand.

Sydney has written about his life in a story which reflects his involvement in human rights for his people, including his time as a guerrilla, living in the Shan jungle.[10]

Chapter 15

Gerry – a ladies' man

Gerry in the 1960s

Gerry, born on 26 April 1943, was a Monday-born. He was the youngest in our family of six so he was called Sai Leik among his family and friends, meaning 'young son'. But he gained the name Gerry at school; again, we have no understanding of where these English names sprang from in the minds of teachers. His official name was Sao Khun Mong Noi, which was my dad's name. The 'Noi' in the name means 'the younger'.

Gerry came into the world during World War II when Burma was under fierce occupation by Japanese troops. Dad was the administrator of Nawng Khio, and at the time of Gerry's birth our home was a busy place. It was the period when our grandmother and my two younger aunts had come to visit us there, and the bridge that connected the town with the main Shan state was bombed, so they were unable to go back to Hsipaw. Then my father's sister, Sao Bo Sawan, and her maids and cook also joined us so we had three houses in our compound. That meant that Gerry had an aunt, a grandmother and our mother to pamper him. Since it was wartime everything was scarce, including milk powder as a substitute for mother's milk, so he was familiar with the taste of honey instead, with our youngest aunt dipping cotton wool into a bowl of honey and squeezing this, drop by drop, into his mouth.

I also recall myself aged about seven, trying to carry Gerry when he was about six months old and losing my grip so that he fell over my shoulder. Then, when Gerry was about four or five he had to use a pair of spectacles and I wondered if it was my fault that his eyesight was harmed from the fall. I also remember an incident in 1945 when the war was almost over. We were in a village being looked after by the township officer when it seemed as if the Allies' paratroopers had dropped from the sky. But the parachutes turned out to be smaller and were sacks of food, such as hard cookies we now call 'dog biscuits', cheese, condensed milk in tubes and tins of sardines. I can still see Gerry tucking in straight from the tin.

After the war, when we were all sent to boarding school, Gerry was left at home as he was still too young to join us. He would tag along when Mum went to the bazaar, often pointing at marshmallows, toffees and chocolates which my soft-hearted mother would buy for him. He was five years old when his older brothers were made Buddhist novitiates in the monastery. Gerry became a little monk just for one day, being disrobed and taken home towards evening as he was too young to stay.

By the time he was about five it was his turn to be sent to the boarding school, Our Lady's Convent in Namtu, and a few years later he joined Sydney at Kambawza College in Taunggyi. Once he was caned by the headmaster for being caught near the girls' hostel. Gerry was acting as a love-letter courier with the intention of delivering a letter to his first cousin from an admirer. So my aunt-in-law, Daw Mi Mi Khaing, wrote to Dad to say it would be best not to send Gerry back to Kambawza, so Dad sent him to St Albert's in Maymyo. He passed his matriculation exam and went on to the University of Rangoon, graduating with a bachelor of law degree. At university he accumulated a lot of girlfriends.

After university, Gerry started working as a medical rep, which meant he had hundreds of samples of painkillers which he had to distribute to doctors. He would play golf with prospective buyers, later managing a lucrative business supplying toilet requisites and groceries to the Japanese who worked for the Mitsubishi company in Rangoon.

He became involved with an actress whose daughter he would drive to school every day. Any jewellery that his relatives asked him to sell would be showered upon this actress. In the end, after receiving diamonds and rubies, she discarded him but held onto the gems.

While playing golf, he met a girl aged just fourteen who became very attached to him. Her mother encouraged her, and they married when she was sixteen and he thirty-six. They had two children, a girl and a boy.

He and his wife were doing very well as they were both ambitious. It's said that it was his idea to send his wife across the border to Bangkok to take care of the business of putting men on board ships as sailors, while he interviewed them in Rangoon for their suitability to the work. Gerry's wife was beautiful and became Miss Indochina, Miss Photogenic and also won another competition as 'best dressed girl'. Thai men couldn't resist chasing after her – and that was the beginning of their marriage break up. She had made a name for herself as a beauty queen, but when someone reported that she was married with two children, she had to give up her titles and all the jewellery that had been showered upon her.

Gerry continued to acquire one singer after another as well as a series of actresses. He had a gift for displaying his possessions and wealth, with jute gunny bags full of money lying against the wall and no accounts whatsoever, so that anyone could snatch one and sneak it out of his house. Later, when he was down and out, no one in our family had enough money to save him.

Gerry lived by his wits. Soon he had set up some business of running trawlers to catch prawns and export them. Some people referred to it as a 'fishy business', thinking they were very clever to make such a joke. By this time, about 1987, we were living in Fiji, so I was mostly unaware of what fortune or misfortune he ran into.

We heard that he would be overloaded with money at one time and down on his luck at another. Once when he was living with a singer, she brought in her brother, then her mother and who knows who else, to share their home. So Gerry was asked to leave his own house. He used to twirl his car chain around his forefinger, and the story goes that after he left the house, the singer called him back in to hand over the car keys to her. So he was left with nothing.

A few years later he married the daughter of his work manager, a woman younger than his own daughter. Gerry was

56 and she was 21. He was never one to be held back by small-minded social conventions: a generous man, giving away anything a person might desire.

In 2005, while living in a fashionable estate in Rangoon, Gerry died suddenly of a heart attack on his way to hospital to seek help.

Travelling with Gerry's son, I went home to Burma, expecting there'd be no one to see to his funeral rites. But the funeral had already been arranged by his ex-sister-in-law and hundreds of friends attended. He was well-known and well-loved.

Chapter 16

Release at last

Khemawadee, Hom and their first-born, Seng, just two years before his 1962 imprisonment

After Hom was released from detention in 1967, the public service commission refused to appoint him to any position on the grounds that he was educationally overqualified. First he answered an advertisement as editor of the government-owned newspaper, *The Working People's Daily*. He was told to go back to university. Then the public service commission said he was overqualified. Later he was appointed a public relations officer to the Burma Red Cross Society, whose chairman was Dr Mg Mg.

Almost two years after Hom was released our third daughter was born, in November 1968. This was seven years after Orawan's birth. The revolutionary government had nationalised the SDA Hospital as a specialist unit, so we registered at the Gandhi Hospital in east Rangoon. My friends warned me that I had made a wrong choice in choosing that hospital because there'd been a mix-up between an Indian baby and a Chin baby, with the parents given the wrong babies. I was relieved to find that it was not a busy afternoon for the maternity ward staff when I went in. There were only two of us in the labour room, an Indian woman and myself, and we had our babies almost simultaneously. There could be no mistake as mine came sliding out on her tummy, with the Mangrai family's trademark lips protruding. She weighed 6 lbs and was almost as tiny as Seng had been. She was a new toy for everyone and her father doted on her. Being a Thursday-born, she was named Maniratana (meaning 'crown jewel'). We called her Ying Awn ('little girl') at home, and she was known as Mani by her friends.

It was a difficult period for us. So my uncle-in-law, Lieutenant Colonel Hla Moe, who as an army officer was a special officer for health and sports, vouched for Hom in seeking employment.

Over the two years since his release, Hom had attended a French class at the institute of languages. In 1973 Hom was recruited by then deputy education minister Dr Nyi Nyi, in the higher education department attached to the ministry of education. Hom was assigned to deal with the UN as head of the UN division. The UNDP wanted Hom to work with the organisation as national program officer, a position that it had advertised in the newspaper. My colleague, the head of department at the University of Rangoon, had a husband who worked for the UNDP. He came over to our house to help Hom fill in the application forms and offered to take them to the UNDP office with Hom's brother the next day.

As I have written earlier, I had approached a monk who was also a psychic and he prayed for Hom to get the UN appointment. He got the job and worked for the UNDP for six years. Soon he was nominated to attend a conference in New York, but, sad to say, the government would not issue a passport for him to travel to the United States.

Burmese parents crave a son, in the belief that by making a son, half of the parent's burden of paying back their own parents' work in nurturing and feeding them is lifted as the boy can become a novice monk. These are the burdens that are carried down the generations, and this form of merit-gaining is believed not to be possible through girl children. At the same time, we cannot belittle girls because it is they who are expected to take on the burden of looking after elderly parents.

I sincerely wanted a son to complete our family, not just for religious merit-making. We already had three girls and Hom's brother had three boys. As Hom's sister-in-law was praying for a little girl, she also prayed for a boy for us. She and Hom's brother were so desperate, they even dressed their second son in girls' clothes. It was funny as he was the most masculine of the three boys. One day when we were at the Great Shwedagon pagoda, Seng pointed to the statue of a goddess who held a little son in her arms. Seng said that she had heard people who wanted a son should pray to that particular goddess. I did that. In 1972, four years after Mani was born, a son was bestowed upon us.

Again I went to the Gandhi Hospital. It was in a sorry state by then because of cutbacks in health services but I had no choice. The other women's hospital was too congested. Fortunately, at the Gandhi Hospital the matron-in-charge was a friend of my Aunty Pansy and Uncle Moe. It was a privilege for me to be given a single room, so I didn't have to worry about any mix-ups of babies. I knew our baby was a boy as soon as he slid out from me, and when the nurse held him up, the same family trademark lips could be seen. We chose his name from a list for Sunday-borns given to me by my dad's youngest brother. Our son was called Sao Ohn Art, meaning 'dignity'. Now everyone calls him Art. At home he is known as Sai Awn (meaning 'little son' in the Shan language) or Thar Gyi (meaning 'big son' in Burmese).

By 1985 Hom was still working for the UN in Rangoon when he was requested by the UNDP headquarters to travel to New York to work there for six months. When he came home in January 1986, he told me that he had been posted to Fiji as an assistant resident representative. Since he had just come home he had his passport in hand.

However, he would have to pay 'educational clearance fees' if he wanted a departure form. This meant that he had to pay K10,000 (US$2,500) for his first degree, a BA (Hons); then another K10,000 for his master of law degree; and finally, another K10,000 for his diploma in French. His records of having been paid a scholarship by the government for these qualifications had been attacked by termites and thrown away. Hom had an affidavit issued stating he had received scholarship money from 1952 to 1956 and found he had to pay that sum too.

He also needed a marriage certificate and a birth certificate for the children. Only then would they let him travel abroad.

Since the children and I were to accompany him, I had to send a letter of resignation to the department of education, and my head of department said she would assist with the procedure to obtain a release order. She took me to the university accounts department where her cousin was in charge, but he was not there. The chief accounts officer who had once worked at the institute of economics was overseas. We had to walk away empty-handed.

Another colleague whose husband was working at the *Burma Socialist Party Magazine* took me to meet her husband who knew an ex-army officer whose workplace was across the river from Rangoon. We took a ferry to see the officer. Since he was at a meeting, he asked us to see him about 3 pm on the Rangoon side of the river. We hired a taxi and all of us – my colleague, her husband, the officer and I - headed to the education minister's house in the suburb of Inya Yeiktha. But the minister and his wife had gone to visit their daughter who was undergoing training at a place called Phaung-gyee where newly appointed government officers had to be trained as members of the Burma Socialist Party, including receiving military training. So the next day we decided to go to the minister's house again, at about ten in the morning. I asked my aunt for the use of her husband's car and their driver to pick up my colleague and her husband, then pick up the military officer and head for the minister's house. The minister had gone to his office, but his wife greeted the officer and he in turn introduced us to her. When I mentioned that I was the niece of U Hla Moe and Daw Khin Ma Lay, she told me that she and her husband had once had the same army posting as my aunt and uncle so they knew each other well. She wanted to know how she could help me. I told her that I had applied for resignation and wanted the release order urgently. She picked up the phone and rang the department of higher education and asked for the officer in charge. This lady was all sweetness to the minister's wife, who asked her what stage my letter of resignation had reached. The lady told her I could see her at 3 pm that day and collect my release order!

It had taken three months to reach this point in receiving the release order. But, believe it or not, after that phone call, we got it that very day. It was up to me to approach desk after desk with boxes of assorted cakes to accelerate the various stages of the processing of this release. In those days it was sufficient to present a pair of sunglasses, a folding umbrella or an Arrow-brand shirt as a sign of appreciation. Nowadays it's a fridge, a car, a gold chain or even a house. I'm happy that I managed to get out when I did. Today I wouldn't be able to afford any of these expensive items.

The next step was to pay a certain amount of money that the taxation office demanded on the future earnings we would receive in Fiji. We didn't have to wait long as the lady in charge of Bank No. 4 in Rangoon had resided in the same hostel as I had at university, and she was happy to speed up the process for us.

Then, at the airport, when we arrived at the place where departure forms were processed, we did not have to queue as we met a friend of our daughter whose father operated the elevator in the building. Isn't it amazing, I thought, that we have to have a special connection to make life easier for us? The lift driver's daughter took us to the officer in charge who sat at a desk looking through our forms. At the same time, the drawer of his desk was open so that we could drop K20 (US$5) for each of us in appreciation of the good deed he was doing.

There wasn't any problem either at the customs immigration desk. We were each allowed to wear one gold chain around our necks and carry $US13 for each adult and US$6.50 for each child less than eighteen years of age.

We had to pay K12,000 (US$3,000) for each of our two older daughters as they had graduated with bachelor of economics and bachelor of commerce degrees. I also had to pay educational clearance fees of K10,000 (US$2,500) for each of my degrees, a bachelor of arts and a master of teaching English as a foreign language.

In those days the US dollar was equal to K4. We were able to pay because when Hom was working in the UN in New York, he saved some money to import a car – a Toyota Hylux – and sell it in Rangoon. This was the trend in those days. When one was sent abroad for further studies, it was a chance to buy a car and bring it back home to trade it. Most of the students would be stressed by the pressure of trying to save for a car as well as study, and this caused them to have 'nervous breakdowns', as they were known. They tried to survive on instant noodles.

We didn't get to see the car as we'd left by the time it arrived in Burma. My cousin said he would help our older girls gain a custom clearance to import the car. Even so, it took some time for the two older daughters and my mother to join us in Fiji. I was so worried to leave the girls behind. One of my daughters especially had a difficult time accepting the UN regulation that it would pay the fares only for children under the age of eighteen, which I knew was reasonable. But we didn't have enough money to take the older girls at that time. I felt sorry for all of us, yet I knew nothing could be done until some time had passed. My mother and my older girls joined us in Fiji one year later.

After five years in Fiji, our son had passed his final examination at high school and wanted to attend the University of NSW in Sydney to study accounting. The UN subsidised his fees for a year and then he went to TAFE to gain a diploma. Our two daughters also wanted to work and could have attended postgraduate courses if we had known that we were going to stay in Fiji for so long, more than five years. Our youngest daughter managed to attend the University of the South Pacific in Suva and graduated with a degree in engineering.

Our youngest daughter joined her brother and sisters in Sydney in 1991. Hom was given an ultimatum by the UN: to choose between taking early retirement or going home to work at the Rangoon UNDP office. Hom chose to retire. By no means were we about to go back to Rangoon.

We had planned to travel as far as Bangkok so that Hom could come out of retirement and accept a job he had been offered in Cambodia. As it was not a safe country at that time, we wanted to have a base in Bangkok so that Hom could come home at weekends.

Then our third daughter was hospitalised in Sydney's Prince Henry Hospital with lupus while we were visiting Sydney. She would require treatment for 15 years, including dialysis for two years, before being offered a donor transplant using one of her brother's kidneys.

Good spirits, in the form of my cousin Gerald and cousin-in-law Cherie, suggested we apply for refugee status in Australia. We did so, the application was accepted, and two years later, in 1996, we became Australian citizens. Only then were we able to travel home to Burma, although my husband has never returned. Once bitten, twice shy.

At least we were able to breathe easily in Australia, and, being citizens, not feel alone as if we were in a foreign country. We felt sorry for our compatriots back home and those waiting for recognition in Australia. For many years I experienced a feeling of disloyalty, as if we had defected, even though in my rational mind I knew it wasn't so.

I've never given up my allegiance to the Shan state within the country of Burma. The truth is we came to Australia from Fiji, after leaving a country under a regime that made normal life almost impossible for most of the population of Burma. We left for the sake of our children's futures, and we were fortunate to have the opportunity of employment in Fiji.

I could not go home to Burma when my mother was ill and dying because, while we were waiting for citizenship, we couldn't obtain travel documents to enter Burma. That hurt me and my mother over the last precious days of her life.

I believed I had been a good daughter to her up until that time. But when my mother passed away, I felt that I had failed her. It would take some years before I could complete my mother's funeral rites. I waited patiently for that day.

Chapter 17

An elopement

Sao Thu Nandar with her husband Sao Ohn Kyar, the second last chief of Hsipaw

My aunt Sao Thu Nandar was nine years older than my mother. As I said, both girls were adopted by their uncle, as their father had died before my mum was born. My aunt's name, meaning 'blessed with good looks', is a Pali word. They were brought up together with eight of their first cousins, including Sao Ohn

Kyar, who married Sao Thu Nandar before he became the chief of Hsipaw state on the death of his father, Sir Sao Khe.

Sao Ohn Kyar was educated in England and obtained a master of arts from Oxford. He was a modern-thinking chief. My mother and other members of the household had to dress up for dinner, and afterwards they would practise ballroom dancing. Sao Ohn Kyar had only one wife to dote on, unlike his father who'd had forty-five wives. Sao Ohn Kyar might have had a roving eye, but he had to acknowledge his wife's youthful beauty and talent. She designed not only her own clothes but also her own palace.

My aunt Sao Thu Nandar in London, 1931

Sao Thu Nandar was especially young and beautiful in the 1930s. My cousin, Nora, another niece of Sao Thu Nandar, described her beauty as 'stunning'. Nora wrote that when Sao Thu Nandar attended the Round Table Conference in 1931, she 'wore a court dress with gloves and a fan of ostrich feathers, together with a brilliant, scintillating diamond headdress made especially for her by the Thai Ayunthian gold artisans of Mandalay. At her entrance everybody turned around to look and there was a silence. She became the centre of attention.'

When the chief returned home, she stayed behind to take treatment for barrenness. After her examination she stayed on, renting a house with my mother, her sister Sao Ohn Nyunt, who was attending a 'finishing school' in London. They had cooking sessions with many Burmese students. Sao Thu Nandar gambled a little and lost. With no money for her return, she had to wait for disbursement of money from home.

When she did return to her husband, the chief, in Hsipaw, she alternated between her summer palace located on the lakeside Sakhanthar (meaning 'pleasant retreat') and a manor house in Maymyo, where the British had developed a hill station. Sao Thu Nandar would go to Maymyo for shopping, but she would reside in Sakhanthar during summer.

The palace at Sakhanthar was built in the second half of the 1920s by Sir Sao Khe. 'He had taken time to find the right spot,' my cousin Nora writes. 'He had wandered about on the hills with elephants until the pleasant site had been chosen.' The palace was a brick building with spires over the chapel. A peacock statue sat on the eastern lintel and a rabbit statue on the west, over the main entrance. Terraced with Italian tiles, broad steps led to the hall which was fully carpeted, with a throne on a dais and decorative carvings behind.

While she was away one summer, some parents presented their daughters to the chief in the Hsipaw palace – and some elders advised him that a chief should have at least four wives. Someone reported this to Sao Thu Nandar, so she ordered her chauffeur to drive her straight home, and she stormed in on the presentation ceremony.

She was haughty and had a temper. The maids did not like her, especially her own maid, the maid of honour as she was called, who was very pretty and whom the chief 'had an eye on', it was said. The maid of honour hoped that one day the chief would also take her as his wife.

At the same time, there was a cousin, Harold, who was madly in love with this maid of honour, and the chief sensed it. He would ask Harold to tour the southern part of Burma during his university holidays. But Harold would cut the tour short, come home and climb a drainpipe to get closer to the maids' quarters, in particular the maid of honour. For his next university holidays, he would be ordered to tour the upper part of Burma. Again he would cut short his tour and come home to climb the drainpipe at night. Eventually Harold married the maid.

Still, my young aunts detected that something was amiss in Mahadevi Sao Thu Nandar's marriage to the chief. There was a male dancer at the court, Sapai Din, his name meaning 'a facial mole', who would entertain the household before dinner. If

Sapai Din was dressed in green, he would wear emerald ear studs, rings and headdress. If he was dressed in a yellow outfit, he had diamond ear studs and rings as well as diamonds in his headdress. The family found that it was their sister who had been showering jewellery upon the dancer. Needless to say, they didn't like him.

After some time, Sao Thu Nandar packed her own jewellery, her clothes, and personal effects, including carpets and her pet dog Mitsy, and left the court to live in the manor in Maymyo. She was accompanied by her dancer, Sapai Din.

Only the Lord above knows why she acted in this frivolous way. She was a queen and the whole of Hsipaw state was proud of her. To others it seemed that she had everything she needed.

News travelled fast. It was a scandal and the chief was devastated.

My grandmother, who was Sao Thu Nandar's mother, and my grandmother's husband were shocked and hurt. My younger aunts and their parents lost face. They moved out of the palace and lived in a house of their own. Sao Thu Nandar was exiled from Hsipaw state.

There was conjecture that she had left because she couldn't love her husband as a wife. He might have felt the same way. They were cousins and they may have only felt cousin love, if there is such a thing. One of my aunts said the maids who had wanted to marry the chief put their heads together and used a kind of voodoo. They dressed a doll to look like Sao Thu Nandar and planted it under her pillows when they made her bed. As a result, she would cry, and roll down the front stairs shouting 'I don't want to stay here! I don't want to stay here!' This was told to me by my young aunt Millie when she visited us in Sydney many years later. She had been young when she'd witnessed what happened in the days before Sao Thu Nandar left the palace and those fateful days afterwards.

The chief took to drink and it's said that he eventually died of a broken heart. His ghost was reportedly seen sitting on a chair under a tree, drinking whisky.

His death left the state with no heir. My father's brother Sao Intra, whom Sir Sao Khe had adopted, had passed away even before the death of Sao Ohn Kyar. But Sao Intra had left a son, Sao Shwe Lu, about two years older than my eldest brother, so he was next in line. After World War II, the trustees of the state tried to contact him to appoint him chief. He thought it was a joke and tore up the letter of appointment. When the chief was on his deathbed he wanted to see his wife, Sao Thu Nandar, perhaps to pass his authority as chief to her, and he also asked to see my grandmother and my father. But the chief's uncles wouldn't allow that to happen.

As for Sao Thu Nandar, she survived living with the moving from place to place with Sapai Din and the dance troupe until the jewellery she had taken was all sold and she became poor. She gave birth to twins, a girl and a boy. The boy died of fever during the Japanese occupation. The girl was placed in a boarding school in Maymyo, where she and I met at the age of about ten, and we became good friends.

After Sao Thu Nandar had left the dancer she worked, given a job by an old friend as manager at the civil supplies department in Myitnge, near Mandalay. She lived there until her younger cousin Charlie was elected chief. He brought her back to Hsipaw, built a house not far from the palace and placed all of his half-sisters under her care. She became like a governess. Later she moved to Rangoon with her daughter and son-in-law.

Sao Thu Nandar was a generous person. She liked to feed people, and she would prepare food every Friday for the student monks who lived across the street from her. She even fed the rats that were living in a hole in the earthen floor with rice that was offered to the Buddha each morning.

She was also known for her sharp tongue. So when my father would call out to his children, 'Would you rather visit your aunt or pull a tiger's tail?', we would answer, 'Pull a tiger's tail.' But she loved me ...

Once Sao Thu Nandar was given a present of a *longyi*, but she didn't like the colour or the design.

'You can't look a gift horse in the mouth,' my mother told her.

'I will – and I'll even look in a horse's arse!' was her retort.

My brothers and I were happy to go for a swim in the stream at the back of her house in Hsipaw, taking the dog, Jimmy, with us. As soon as Jimmy would see the geese swimming in the stream he would chase them, my brothers calling out to encourage him until my aunt would come out of her house to stop the ruckus.

One day after our swim we walked home and changed our clothes as usual, and a few hours later my aunt and her maid came to our house. The maid was carrying something in a basket and my brothers asked what was in it. My aunt replied, 'The goose you set Jimmy to chase and attack died after you left, so I've cooked it for you.' I wouldn't eat it, as I'm finicky about food.

I can also remember another time when she chased me around the house to drink castor oil, calling out, 'Biddy, come back. I've made it palatable, I've cured the smell.'

‘Come and have it,’ she coaxed. I relented and quickly gulped it down.

She used to give her daughter Gladys and me castor oil once a month as a laxative, which I detested. I preferred to take Epsom’s salts which the nuns dispensed with a piece of jaggery, or palm sugar, which they popped into our mouths. In those ‘olden days’, our elders thought it was essential for us to take what was referred to as an ‘opening dose’ every month.

By the 1970s, Sao Thu Nandar was very happy whenever I dropped in to see her after work – and there was always something prepared beforehand for me to eat. A grilled fish stuffed with spring onions, coriander, chilli and Shan spices, and wrapped in banana leaves, before being grilled on wood fire ambers or a charcoal stove, was a favourite of mine. She would also make strawberry toffee or guava cheese.

Sao Thu Nandar passed away at the age of 95 in the 1990s while we were living in Fiji. I always regret that I was not there to help her at the end or able to attend her funeral due to the political conditions at that time, which did not allow me to travel to and from my home country freely.

The Sakandar Summer Palace, built by Hsipaw prince Sir Sao Khe in the early 1900s, now lies derelict and unnoticed just off the road used by tourists

Chapter 18

Lily of the Heavens

My aunt Sao Bo Sawan

The town of Kengtung, in the eastern Shan states, was enclosed by mud brick walls for five miles around it. Near the centre of the enclosure was the chief's palace, the *haw*. A paved road led up an incline to the front gate which was the place where that uncle of mine, a Shan chief, had been assassinated in 1937 by his nephew. As a child I would enter the grounds, which were enclosed by six-foot-high brick walls, and would walk along to a two-storey house where my aunt whose name meant 'lily of the heavens' or 'lotus', Sao Bo Sawan, used to live – just as my grandmother and great grandmother had lived there before her. Behind the house was a lake with lotuses.

The palace itself was made of bricks and was painted white and the roof was made of corrugated zinc sheets and brick red tiles. There were polished timber floors and marble passageways. The palace had French windows and two turrets with cupolas on them, perhaps at odds with my grandfather's alternative ideas inspired by the Indian architecture he saw when he attended a durbar in India, an official meeting of the rulers of the Shan states with the British government in the early twentieth century.

As soon as you stepped inside, you would find yourself in a huge hall. Staircases to the right and the left of this hall took you to the upper level. All was destroyed by the military.

Kengtung haw (palace)

I still see my aunt standing at one of the French windows gazing at what goes on at and around the building that once belonged to her father, the 41st chief of Kengtung state before he was assassinated. She was his third daughter and my father's younger sister.

I see her smoking cigarette after cigarette which she holds as no one else does, between her third and ring fingers. Whatever she does, she does it with grace. She looks elegant and carries her tall and slender self as befits her status as the chief's daughter. She's also charming and witty.

Lily of the Heavens is fair-skinned and has thick, jet-black, ankle-length hair and thick eyebrows. She remains single all her life, seeming to take pride in it. She brushes off any suitor who asks for her hand in marriage. It seems to me that she loves only herself and material possessions.

Lily likes hoarding so much that by the time of the military coup, she has almost everything the military dictatorship has stopped people from importing: beverages, dried fruits, and ancient statues of the Buddha, which she keeps under lock and key. She even has a generator ready for use as soon as the electricity is cut off. She needs it since she needs water pumped to the residence. The old man who used to operate the manual pump had died. I remember an elderly relative commenting, 'Sao, your aunt will become a mouse in her next existence, she is such a hoarder.'

My earliest memories are that my aunt liked to display her latest acquisitions, especially jewellery. My brother was six when he saw a small pistol she kept under her pillow for protection. He thought it was a toy.

'Sao Ar [Aunty] would you give it to me?' he asked.

'You may have it when I die.'

I was aged about four then. She thrust out her hand and showed me her diamond bracelet and asked me, 'Is it pretty?'

'Yes, would you give it to me?' I answered. But she only repeated, 'You may have it when I die.'

From that day on, my brother and I would go to her room every day to ask 'Sao Ar, aren't you dead yet?'

Apart from the jewellery she wore, Lily sent the best and the most precious pieces to her younger brother across the border in Chiang Mai. Her most trusted housekeeper carried them for her. She had accumulated so much wealth that she didn't know where to keep it all. She placed the rest of her jewellery in a metal sea chest and had a gardener bury it under a tamarind tree. When she passed away, the trustees had a hard time before they located it, as the gardener she had entrusted to bury the chest had died before her.

There were numerous tamarind trees, loganberry, sugar maple, lime and star apple trees in the backyard. The silos in the huge barn were full of paddy with husk and white rice. Next to the barn there was a well from which the water was pumped up. Beyond the well was a rear fence with a small gate to get through to the lake, which had a wealth of pink and purple water lilies to gaze upon. There were boat races every year conducted by the chief administrator. Across the lake were orange and mandarin groves. My aunt knew how to be self-sufficient.

In my memory, sometimes as she stands there at the window, she calls out a greeting to a person whose father once served her nephew, the chief. Then she throws a barrage of curses on him. She cannot accept that a person who had worked for the chief is now working for the Burmese government. From her window she sees soldiers climbing coconut trees that line the driveway. She shouts out, 'Hey, what are you doing up there?'

A soldier replies, 'Picking coconuts.'

'Oh, do you have parents who need coconuts as offerings?', my aunt throws back at him.

It is at this window that she may have recalled the grandeur of the palace and the glorious days of her father's rule, and then the pain of her heartbroken mother, whose niece her father had taken as his sixth and youngest wife. She may have witnessed the appointment of her eldest brother as the next chief after her father's death. Who knows what went on in her mind? She may have recalled the night of 22 October 1935 when her brother, the forty-second chief, was murdered on the sloping ground at the front gate. She and her younger sister were walking one step behind him on their way to the palace to host an end of Lent dinner and festivity after having attended a religious ceremony at the monastery. It may never have entered her mind that someone might be so audacious as to come forward and shoot the chief with a bullet made of gold. Such a golden bullet befits a chief and indicates the intent of assassination. It may have been even harder for her to accept the truth that her nephew, the son of her eldest sister by another mother, was the culprit. How could one deny that sibling rivalry wasn't rife in a situation where six wives and nineteen children existed. There was bound to be jealousy between two half-brothers – born only seven days apart – especially when one of them thought he was the rightful heir to the chieftainship as he was the principal wife's son.

Do I detect tears rolling down her cheeks, now she is ageing, as she stands at her favourite window? Has she ever regretted not marrying? Three of her sisters were married off to three different chiefs. They call these 'marriages of alliance'. Has she forgiven her younger brother for fleeing the country across the border to live with his Thai wife and family, leaving her, alone and aged, with the housekeeper? This housekeeper, whom we all regarded as my aunt's adopted daughter, did the shopping, cleaning and cooking in between midwifery. When she went on these trips, she would lock my ageing aunt inside, let four Alsatian dogs out into the yard and ride her bicycle to do her work. She too had accumulated wealth. Unlike her mistress, she kept all her jewellery in potties with lids under her bed. Electricity was supplied only between 7 pm and 10 pm, so ironing and many other chores had to be done within this strict time limit. After 10 o'clock every night she would talk loudly to herself so that people would think there were more than two people in the house.

She had one of her nieces, a young girl, come over to sleep with my aunt at night to keep her warm in winter. During the day, the little girl would run up and down the stairs on errands until she went to school at 3 pm. She soon became bored as she was only allowed to leave my aunt's bedside to go to the toilet. A bell was placed at the bedside table for my aunt to ring if she needed something, and sometimes the little girl would hardly even have reached the stairs when the bell would ring again. So one day she removed the clapper inside the bell so she could take a longer break. My aunt tried to use the bell and no sound was heard. She wanted to laugh as well as scold the little girl. It was just one of the many hopeless situations that my aunt had to face towards the end of her life.

In one way at least, she had prepared for the day she would have to face death. If death should come, then who would do the traditional rituals according to the Khun custom, she wondered? So she made velvet pillows, velvet cushions, patchwork quilts in threes, fives and sevens, the auspicious odd numbers, ready to be offered to the monastery so that she wouldn't have to go without them in the next life. She even dressed up plastic dolls in miniature Kaw costumes of a hill tribe in order that she might have servants when reincarnated. She was very good at handicraft – weaving, knitting, embroidering and sewing.

But what had my aunt done in a previous existence to deserve such a fate as the parlous state she was in before her death, I wonder?

Chapter 19

A golden umbrella

My cousin Maung Maung (front row centre) in a novitiation ceremony, late-1950s

A teaching colleague one day scathingly remarked that I had never forgotten the half day of glory when I wore clothes that resembled Shan royal attire. I was showered with money and jewellery as I walked along with my family during a procession at a Buddhist novitiating ceremony for my brother. We had golden umbrellas held above our heads

The ceremony is held when a boy turns ten and parents prepare him to be a novitiate, or little monk. At the same ceremony small girls are dressed up as princesses to have their ears pierced. This usually takes place during the school summer holidays when it is hot weather and the monasteries, built under a canopy of large trees, provide some relief from the heat for the boys and their families.

Another good reason for the novitiation ceremonies to be held during the summer school break is that it keeps the boys out of trouble as they are confined to the monastery and its compounds under the care and guidance of the older monks. The boys are taught the correct way to ask the senior monks for saffron robes about a month or two before the set date. They have their heads shaved and are bathed before being adorned with the saffron attire, which includes vest-like singlets, sarongs and girdles made of twisted cotton string used to secure the sarongs in place. Robes are used to keep their bodies covered and warm when the weather is cooler. The boys are also provided with alms bowls to receive food as they walk around the village every day. A piece of cloth for distilling water to ensure that they don't swallow insects or worms is also included in the prerequisites, together with a razor blade for shaving the head, and the last requirement, a needle and thread. These are the eight items only that a monk should have.

Monks have early morning breakfast at 5 or 6 am, lunch at about 11 and nothing to eat until the next morning. They have to keep the ten precepts of refraining from: killing living creatures; stealing; telling lies; drinking alcohol; sexual activity; taking meals after noon; luxury, such as sleeping on an ornate bed; singing, dancing and watching entertainments; wearing flowers; holding cash or gold.

The boys have to learn to recite prayers. It's a hard life for little boys who are used to running wild or those who have been pampered by parents.

My nephew, who is about the same age as my son, was not accustomed to a squatting type of toilet. After five days at the monastery he started to vomit so his mother took him home. When I visited my son, taking lunch for the monks and the novices, he cried when he saw me – but he managed to stay there for the required ten days.

Coming to think more deeply about it, I ask myself is it fair to have the boys novitiated in this way? Can they understand what they are doing and why? Is the meritorious deed beneficial for the parents only, or for the little boys too? When my son turned twelve, before we left for Fiji, he agreed to go into a novice's life again. This time I believe he understood the whole process and learnt to be a good Buddhist, saying his prayers regularly right up until the present day.

The colleague who'd remarked scathingly that I had never forgotten the half a day of glorification, having that golden umbrella above my head at the novitiating ceremony, had meant to shame me. She meant that I hadn't forgotten the life I had lived before Burma's coup d'etat in 1962. Yet how could I?

My life might be likened to a sturdy tree, at first developed through the nurturing of a seedling, then a sapling, with love and care. It was ready to spread out its branches and reach up towards the sky. It was ready to produce fragrant flowers and fruits to feed other beings, to support twittering birds dropping seeds to the ground to once again spring roots and sprout shoots for new lives.

Who wouldn't have missed a life that was full of hope and ambition? Hom and I had been married just three years and eight months – we had the promise of many fulfilling years ahead – when suddenly that tree of life was struck by lightning. It's lucky it wasn't killed altogether. Slowly, ever so slowly, while we were separated by his imprisonment yet still together in spirit, tender leaves started to appear along that tree trunk, signalling that it was still but barely alive. Our struggle to regain the right to live freely together was challenging – not so challenging as to have us beg, borrow or steal, but challenging in so many other ways, in enduring hardship every day.

The Lord Buddha and the guardian angels didn't ignore us. Parents, relatives and friends supported us. We didn't wallow in sorrow. We didn't crave for what might have been. It was my duty to keep my family intact: to feed them, to clothe them, to give them an education and to keep them happy. Why should they suffer? They hadn't asked to be born into this family.

At least my children learnt to fend for themselves. When Orowan was two or three years old, I would carry her as I walked our eldest daughter, Seng, to school. It was one street away from where we were staying with my parents on Signal Pagoda Road, and little boys would dance around us and tease Orowan calling her a midget. She would reach down from my arms and hit the boys' heads with her chubby hand. I would encourage her, saying '*ch-tha-cha, na-na-cha,*' meaning 'hit hard'.

Years later, when Seng and Orowan were about 18 and 16, I sent them to the market, asking them to buy some flowers for the altar. A man followed them and called out to Orawan '*chit chit, chit chit,*' meaning 'lovey dovey'. Seng spun around and punched the man with all her strength. An altercation took place while an elderly man tried to calm her down. She asked the mediator what he would have done if his own daughter was called 'lovey dovey'. Seng learnt to protect her sister.

One day I was at my desk in the English department of the University of Rangoon when a senior clerk came to me saying that he needed help as my daughter was involved in a fight. It was Seng again, fighting with two boys who were throwing stones at her and her friend. When I arrived at the scene she was whirling her Shan bag round and round above her head to ward off the stones. As soon as the boys saw the staff arriving, they took off in their car. Seng saw the number plate and knew at once that it used to belong to her grand uncle, so she managed to trace the owner and reported the incident to the police. Since the boys were about to board a ship to work for a shipping line, they were barred from boarding as they had a police case pending. The outcome was that they had to apologise personally to Seng, and she had to have the case dropped so the boys could board the ship. I've taken pride in my children successfully defending themselves.

In Burma people talk about how they waged war on the British, how they fought for independence, how they banished the Japanese, how they subdued many Karen rebels, how they repelled some Kachin guerrillas, how they fought against the Shan and how they pushed back the Chinese Kuomintang troops.

What is never mentioned is how we wives of the detainees during the 1962 military coup were forced to fight our own war. Did we dare fight? We were so afraid of doing more harm, which could jeopardise the release of our husbands, that we didn't dare utter a word. Two of the internees' wives went underground, taking their children with them. Another had a heart attack and fell down dead in her bathroom, leaving eight daughters ranging from age ten to twenty-four to fend for themselves. Yet another wife had to leave the country, taking her two little girls as her life had been made so miserable by the guards placed at her gates. Later we learnt that her husband, who was my mother's cousin, was murdered instead of being kept under custody by the military. Another detainee's wife, my husband Hom's aunt-in-law, was ordered to leave the country within a week of her husband's imprisonment.

How were we to survive when our bank accounts were frozen? How could we live when most of us depended on our husbands for sustenance? That was the time when I had to take up the challenge. At least I was qualified to teach, so I could earn an income.

I, who was so shy as a girl and young woman that I used to cry when I was asked to face the class and read, I who would weep when asked to give an impromptu talk! This young woman now had to face fifty students, then a hundred, and later two hundred, in lectures. How did I manage this? Only God knows.

Yet you'll recall that when I was young I spoke so softly that my father used to say, 'Louder, Biddy, louder!' Not understanding, I would repeat after him, 'Louder. Louder'. It became a standing joke in our family. Little did I know that later in life I would need to speak up for myself and my children, to nurture and protect them when my husband was unjustly imprisoned for five years. So my father was right. Could he have foreseen the strength I would need to face the horror of my life ahead? Having endured so many hardships himself, and speaking his thoughts out loudly, he might have been paving a way for us, his children, to follow the right path stoically, as he had done.

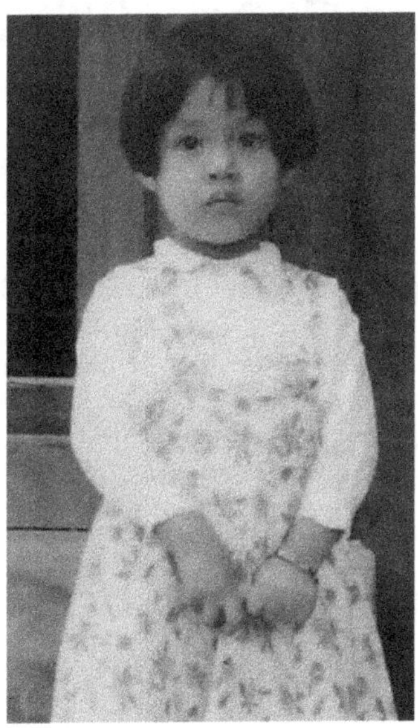

Khemawadee aged five

Chapter 20

My journey home

A pagoda in Hsum Hsai built by my ancestors

It was a journey that led down memory lane, but a journey filled with expectancy as well as nostalgia. There were ten of us from Sydney on the trip in November 2012, first visiting Thailand and then home to Myanmar.

My son, Sao Ohn Art, decided to celebrate his marriage to Liyuan Zhang at Wat Ku Tao monastery in Chiang Mai. He had arranged with my brother Sydney – now known as Singhadej and living in Bangkok – to offer food to the Shan monk and other monks residing in Chiang Mai.

So we flew from Bangkok to Chiang Mai and were met by my brother's friend who had an eleven-seater van, which he used to drive us first to our hotel and then wherever we wished to go. He provided superb service for us and even cooked the meal for the monks.

Of special interest to us was a place where there were statues of the three kings of ancient Chiang Mai, among them our ancestor, King Mangrai, who'd crossed the Mekong River to conquer the Wa people and found the Kengtung state. We were excited to see the gilt-covered bronze statues, erected in the 13th century, as we felt a connection with this power.

King Mangrai is fabled to have been born of parents sent from the spirit world, while the Wa aborigines of the country are supposed to have sprung from the soil. The king lived in a tiered building and had several hundred wives, who in the late afternoon would go out on elephant-back to bathe in the river. No doubt there was quite an intermingling of the races.

We also visited the place where the king is said to have spent his last days, marked by a marble monument standing upon his tomb, with his history inscribed on it in Thai. King Mangrai is said to have died after he was struck by lightning. We Burmese and Shan believe that lightning strikes only those who have done something wicked, but the king had negotiated peace between the other two warring kings so he could have been someone who had done good deeds. It might have been the metal or gold regalia that he had adorned himself with that attracted the lightning.

In Yangon, the city I'd known for so long as Rangoon, I stayed first with my mother's youngest sister, Aunty Pansy, which is one house away from my cousin Naomi, Aunty Millie's daughter. One day Naomi picked us up early in her van and there were seven of us travelling together. With me were my eldest daughter Seng and her friend Pyar Li, our youngest daughter Maniratana, Naomi and myself, and her driver.

We set off for Maymyo one hundred and fifteen miles away, intending to have breakfast there. We drove past the airport at Mingaladon, and Htaukyant, the site of a war cemetery – places so different from when I was a girl. Then we were on the highway and hungry, so we decided to eat at a resting place on the way. We ordered breakfast of traditional Burmese rice in fish soup, fried rice with steamed peas, and glutinous rice cooked in oil, to go with small fried fish and tea or coffee. We chose not to have the curries or dried fried meat as my youngest daughter was not feeling well. She was not bothered about the food, instead asking for wi-fi at every meal stop we made.

Eventually we reached Aneesakhan where my mother's eldest niece, Gladys, lives. She had prepared high tea, and rice noodles and chicken to go with it. She had beds ready for us to sleep the night, but we declined and, after the meal, we set forth for Maymyo again, taking Gladys along with us.

There, we checked in at a hotel, staying in small cottages, and we had breakfast in a large dining hall. Everything seemed so new and neat since my last visit to the town sixty years before. One thing that remained as beautiful as ever was the botanic garden, especially its pond filled with pink, purple and white lotuses.

We then proceeded to Nawng Khio where my father had worked as an administrator. Soon I had some apprehension as to the driver's skill, since I knew we were about to descend hairpin bends that my father had deftly manoeuvred for so many years. The roads that the British had built were meant for driving on the left-hand side of the road. But after 1962, General Ne Win ordered that cars be driven on the right-hand side of the road. At least these roads were wider now, so that even two ten-wheeler trucks can avoid each other round the bends. Generally an etiquette applies for drivers going uphill to give way to those travelling downhill. As we ascended, I could see the famous Goakhteik Bridge over a deep ravine high above us. Eventually we were on our way to Hsipaw, my birthplace, and by now I had confidence in the driver even though he had never driven to the Shan states.

Roadside stalls sold all kinds of garden produce: bananas, dragon fruit, oranges and mandarins. On sale were tofu crackers, rice crackers, pickled pork, rice cakes made out of black glutinous rice and round sesame seeds, fried tofu, and milk crackers. Also sold were wooden triangular blocks with handles to stop the car from rolling backwards.

Our destination was the famous Baw Gyo pagoda, where festivals are held every year. Ever since the days of the first chiefs, it's been a place where Burmese and Shan have brought their wares to sell. The pagoda was built at the spot where a Shan princess was met by her father on her return home after her husband, the king of Burma, was said to have ordered her home for being a witch because she had ears that sparkled. Actually it was her diamond earrings that sparkled, reflecting light, which other consorts had reported to the king as witchcraft to create false fears. The pagoda itself is guarded by invisible living beings, represented by the statues of five ogres – a father and four sons. When my uncle – the chief – ascended the throne, it was too burdensome a duty to keep them guarding the summer palace at Sakhanthar, where they were fed about four kilos of beef every day. So he moved them, together with their statues, to this pagoda. To us they didn't look ferocious. They almost smiled at us.

After we had said our prayers and showed our merits with the living, the dead and the spirits, we made our way to Hsipaw town. On the way we could see the summer palace in ruins, with only its four pillars remaining, and the burial place of the chiefs in ruins too. It was a sad sight. On the roadside there were two statues of racehorses which had belonged to my aunt, erected when they'd died. The villagers believed that the horses had become spirits and made a spirit house for them, worshipping and paying respects!

We reached the Hsipaw monastery just after lunchtime and the presiding abbot was waiting to welcome us. He had our beds ready in a hall that had a dining area, a toilet and a bathroom attached. He also had a huge hot pot prepared for our lunch. As my cousin Naomi did not eat pork, the monk stir-fried some vegetables for her. There were volunteers who cooked, served, washed up the plates and cups, and even made our beds. The hall had sofas and coffee tables but they were pushed to one corner to make room for our bedding on the floor. The beds were made of a carpet, a thin mattress, a bedspread and two pillows each, with new towels laid out for our use. We felt so important and so special here in my home town again.

The abbot was a nephew of one of our grandfather's forty-five wives. He treated us as his cousins, with warmth and respect. He had covered the walls of the monastery with historical photographs which were striking and new to our eyes, particularly two large photos of a reigning group of Shan state chiefs from the 19th century. The light was bad and my camera had run out of battery charge, so my eldest daughter Seng had to wait for the morning light to take her own shots of the photos. There were also many photos of my aunt, who was the Mahadevi of Hispaw, wearing various national costumes. She was beautiful in whatever she wore. My grandmother's portrait was there, and I now wish I had taken it home with me when the abbot said that I could. He said there were more photographs in the next building but we did not go over as it was raining. Again, I wish I had gone. But we had to go back to the spirit house outside Hsipaw because at eight o'clock the next morning we would pray and offer bananas and flowers to the spirits there before returning to Maymyo.

Before breakfast was served, the abbot came over to the building where we'd been housed and sat at a place where he used to sit before the lay people. I couldn't sit on the floor, so I sat on a chair opposite him while I asked about my grandfather and his older brother, Sao Khe. He said they were close brothers and the rumours spread about my grandfather's desire to revolt against him were not true. I was relieved to hear about it. The other brother, Sao O, was a half-brother and he was appointed chief by the Japanese occupation. While we were at the monastery we met our grand uncle Sao O's younger son from a 'much lesser' wife. His wife was a teacher and was one of the ladies who was helping to do the daily chores at the monastery.

I also met my mother's cousin who was the same age as Aunty Millie. Now she is 97 and until recent years gave English tuition to the local students. She used to be the headmistress of the state high school. I was exhilarated to see my playmate while visiting Aunty Muriel in Sao Myo Set. We visited the Haw of the palace that my aunt Sao Thu Nandar designed and her husband the chief Sao Ohn Kyaar had built for her. The grounds were overgrown with weeds. Some flowers were struggling to stay alive. The summer house that we used to play in looked as if it was going to fall sideways anytime.

The house where we used to live in after the war, the house where Tim and Sydney were born, still looked the same. My grandmother's house and my aunt Sao Thu Nandar's house in town are still there. The new owners haven't done any renovations that I could see.

We made our way back to the Goakhteik gorge and bridge, heading for Wet Wun, Ohnmathee, Ohnmakha – towns once so familiar to me as places where special rices could be bought, and now so changed – and then May Mgo where we had lunch at a garden restaurant with huts. As it was drizzling outside, we couldn't walk around the gardens.

When we reached Mandalay to rest for the night, it was still raining. The hotel had timber furniture and marble bathrooms, and a one-slab teak coffee table top reminded me of my father's dining table. We went to see the pagoda built by my maternal grandmother's ancestors but the inscriptions were no longer visible. The next morning my two daughters who were travelling with me went at 4 am to witness the face-washing ceremony of the Buddha's statue at the famous Maha Myat Muni pagoda.

Then we headed back to Yangon, staying at Nay Pyi Daw, the new capital that the military government had built, in a luxurious hotel that comprised a cluster of cottages. I thought about how we would not have been able to travel and stay in these hotels if we'd been on our own. My cousin paid for everything.

I needn't have had the jitters about the state of the roads nor the condition of the toilets in the new Burma. It was a wonderful journey in many ways, despite my sadness about all that had been lost. November was school holiday break and at times I felt as I used to on my way home for holidays more than sixty years ago. The same scenery caught my eye: the yellow carpets of sesame fields with wild sunflowers enhancing the hue.

However, the trip would end with mixed feelings of joy and sadness. The visit to the haw, or palace, had left me in sorrow. It was occupied by the son of my mother's cousin, Sao Kyar Zone, brother to Sao Kyar Saing, the last chief of the Hsipaw state.

General Ne Win's henchmen had taken Sao Kyar Saing into custody and it is believed he was murdered by them in 1962. My aunty-in-law, his widow, now lives in the United States with her two daughters because living in Burma was made impossible for them by the regime, as it was also made impossible for my family.

She, Sao Thu Santi or Inge Sargent, was an Austrian who adapted herself to the Shan and the Burmese ways of life when she married. She spoke both Shan and Burmese. The love she had for the people and cultures of these lands was evident when she lived there, and was reflected again in her writing of her biography.[11]

We all share regrets over the losses we have suffered which, day by day, we have learned to live with but not accept.

I can only hope that the story I have set out here of my life in Burma – a life that I had to give up abruptly – will throw some light on the terrible ordeals that thousands of Burmese, Shans and people of other ethnic groups have also endured. Their troubles – stretching from the period of the British and then Japanese colonial occupations through to the 1962 military dictatorship which still retains power – have not gone away but persist to this day.

I pray that my story of the past glories and the perils that remain for ethnic minorities and the Burmese alike might reach across the world into the hearts of people who can step forward to assist all the people of the country now known as Myanmar.

Water blessing at Shwe Dagon pagoda

[1] 'Shan princess 'returns' to Myanmar', *The Myanmar Times*, 13-19 June 2011, www.mmtimes.com/2011/timeout/579/timeout57901.html

[2] There is a parable about the Kankucho bird that shivers from cold because it has not built a nest in good times and as a result suffers during winter. The story symbolises how human thoughts fluctuate and people often take the line of least resistance. Perhaps that is the meaning of the sound I heard, perhaps not.

[3] For a thorough discussion of the 1947 assassinations see Kin Oung, *Who Killed Aung San?* White Lotus Company, Bangkok 1993.

[4] Sai Aung Tun, *History of The Shan State*, Silkworm Books Chiang Mai 2009 p 363.

[5] *ibid* p 346.

[6] Yuwadi Khin Sein Hlaing, *Shwe Hlan Bo* (*Commander of the Golden Lance Brigade),* Swedaw Press Yangon 2004.

[7] Kin Oung, *Who Killed Aung San?* White Lotus Bangkok 1993 raises questions about who may have been the 'masterminds' behind the actions of the assassin convicted of the murders.

[8] Mi Mi Khaing, *Burmese Family*, Bloomington, Indiana University Press 1946 & 1962; *Cook and Entertain the Burmese Way*, Karoma Publishers Ann Arbor 1978;*The World of Burmese Women,* Zed Press, London 1984.

[9] Chao Tzang Yawnghwe, *The Shan of Burma: Memoirs of a Shan Exile*, Institute of Southeast Asian Studies Singapore, 1987.

[10] *A Cat Has Nine Lives*, unpublished.

[11] Inge Sargent, *Twilight over Burma – My Life as a Shan Princess*, University of Hawaii Press, 1994

www.ingramcontent.com/pod-product-compliance
Lightning Source LLC
La Vergne TN
LVHW010611110826
845149LV00003B/863

* 9 7 8 0 9 9 4 5 4 4 1 8 6 *